I can think in Spanish and write in Spanish. I can think in English and write in English.

From Ideas to Words

I used to write just a little English. now I know lots and lots.

I didn't know I had poems inside of me.

Writing Strategies for English Language Learners

i keep this notebook with me all the time. it's got wheek and ENGLISH!

It feels like freedom when I write in Korean

TASHA TROPP LAMAN

Heinemann
Portsmouth, NH

Heinemann
361 Hanover Street
Portsmouth, NH 03801–3912
www.heinemann.com

Offices and agents throughout the world

The author and publisher wish to thank those who have generously given permission to reprint borrowed material:

Figure 1.1 from *Time for Meaning: Crafting Literate Lives in Middle & High School* by Randy Bomer. Copyright © 1995 by Randy Bomer. Published by Heinemann, Portsmouth, NH. Reprinted with permission.

Credits continue on page iv.

Library of Congress Cataloging-in-Publication Data
Laman, Tasha Tropp.
 From ideas to words : writing strategies for English language learners / Tasha Tropp Laman.
  pages cm
 Includes bibliographical references and index.
 ISBN-13: 978-0-325-04360-9
 1. English language—Rhetoric—Study and teaching—Foreign speakers. 2. English language—Study and teaching—Foreign speakers. 3. Academic writing—Study and teaching. 4. Second language acquisition. I. Title.

PE1128.A2L37 2013
808'.042071—dc23   2013001582

Editor: Margaret LaRaia
Production: Victoria Merecki
Typesetter: Kim Arney
Cover and interior designs: Bernadette Skok
Back cover photo: Bob Laman
Manufacturing: Steve Bernier

Printed in the United States of America on acid-free paper.
17   16   VP   2   3   4   5

This book is written in memory of

Dorothy M. Menosky
Richard E. Ransburg
Jennifer L. Wilson

Contents

Acknowledgments

Thank you to the many teachers whose teaching shines on these pages. For the last sixteen years, I've had the great fortune to learn with and from the dedicated work of so many teachers through study groups, writing institutes, coaching, and school collaborations in Belize, Central America, New Mexico, Indiana, and now South Carolina. I am grateful for their trust in me and for their feedback on early drafts of my writing. I am a better teacher because of each of them. Where permitted, I have used teachers' names. For those teachers whom I could not name, I am grateful for your time, energy, and endless enthusiasm for teaching. Thank you for letting readers into your classrooms so that others may learn with and from you.

Thanks to the multilingual children whose ideas and words dance on these pages; they are my daily inspiration to keep growing and learning. I am grateful to their families for supporting this work and their children.

My colleagues in the Department of Instruction and Teacher Education at the University of South Carolina are the most supportive colleagues I could wish for. A special shout out to Amy Donnelly and Ken Vogler, who took over my role as Elementary Program Coordinator so that I could pursue writing this book with complete devotion. Thanks to my graduate assistants, who helped me with research and the final tasks of pulling this book together: Kirsten Wade, Amber Hartman, and Jamie Yobs.

Pamela C. Jewett, Tambra O. Jackson, and Kara Brown are some of my most trusted colleagues, friends, and writing partners. They read drafts of chapters and helped me clarify my ideas. I also thank Pamela C. Jewett for sharing her resources for the appendices. Thanks to Lucy Spence for suggesting that I write this book, and thanks to my friend and mentor, Heidi Mills, for her constant support, friendship, and interest in this project.

Before moving to South Carolina, I studied at Indiana University where I grew my knowledge base about literacy in general and about writing workshop in particular. Randy Bomer invited me to teach at the Indiana Partnership for Young Writers Summer Institute. Because of Randy and the current director, Susan Adamson, I had the opportunity to learn with some of the finest writing educators in the country, if not the world, including both of them.

Thanks to Isoke Titilayo Nia for sharing her thinking and teaching and for letting me share her framework for planning in this book. This book happened because Carl Anderson asked me, "What book are you going to write, Tasha?" He also shared my idea with Heinemann when I was too scared to even consider talking to a publisher. Katherine Bomer has been a generous mentor and friend from near and far. Her books, *Writing a Life* and *Hidden Gems*, spearhead the need for human response and connection when teaching writers, and they have informed my thinking and my work with teachers and multilingual writers.

Thanks to my Indiana University teachers and friends who first supported my research and my work with multilingual students: Mitzi Lewison, Jerome C. Harste, Carolyn Burke, Phil F. Carspecken, and Bradley Levinson. Thanks to Amy Seely Flint and Katie Van Sluys for their continued collaboration and constant friendship.

I feel as if I won the writing lottery by having Margaret LaRaia as my editor. I saved every draft of this book and every email from her because her keen insight, warm comments, and brilliant suggestions helped me clarify my thinking and taught me as much about writing as they did about teaching writers. Zoë Ryder White, another fantastic teacher and editor also gave me writing support. Zoë's poetic eye and enthusiasm could keep a writer going and going and going. The production team at Heinemann did a gorgeous job on this book and I am grateful to Bernadette Skok who designed the beautiful cover and created the interior design. Elisia Brodeur's careful copyediting made a tremendous difference. Thanks to Victoria Merecki, production editor, whose eye for detail and attention to design are a writer's dream.

Much of this book is about the communities we create in classrooms and how we shape—and are shaped by—the communities to which we belong. I live on a street where a supportive community is right outside my front door. I want to thank all of my Pinewood friends, with special thanks to Kathleen Robbins for her frequent front-porch coffee breaks, title consultation, and interest in this project; Angela Marterer for being the dearest friend ever; both of their respective husbands, Benjamin Madden and Aaron Marterer, for early morning runs before long days of writing; and Darcy Freedman and Heath Blackard, for evening strolls and writing conversations. And thanks to all of the children on my street: Lenora, Genevieve, Asher, Miles, and Tate, who got me out of my chair to play.

Someone once told me that the world can grow bigger or smaller when you are grieving. Most of this book was written during great heartache after my dear friend and colleague Jennifer Wilson was murdered. But in the days, weeks, and months following this tragedy, so many people came forward to hold me up, listen, and just be there in that darkest season of my life. I witnessed the miracle and healing effects of everyday kindnesses. Thank you to Annie Wright, Stacey Millner-Collins, Erin Miller, Susi Long, and Jemme Stewart for reminding me that even when there is darkness there is still light.

I was fortunate to be born into and then marry into families that fill my life with love, purpose, and stories. My mom and stepfather, Karen and Andy Carter, and my father, Richard Tropp, have always loved and believed in me. My sister, Stephanie Tropp Deetsch, is my best friend, and my brother James Tropp's frequent texts—asking me if I was writing—kept me honest. Benjamin Deetsch and Aya Sarmiento Tropp, their spouses, are my newest siblings, and I adore them. My grandmother, Imojewel Ransburg, baked me a rhubarb pie just before this book was due; I am convinced that helped me finish!

Thanks to Shirley and Ted Kriefall, who let me take over their dining room table for a week while I worked on this book. Shirley's gift boxes of books were my favorite distraction while writing my own. My sisters- and brothers-in-law: Kathy and Chris Cognasso and Jennifer and Jay Holmes are my west coast siblings, and I thank them for supporting me all these years. My father-in-law, Robert Laman Sr., always sends cards just when I need them most. My nephews and nieces are my favorite people in the world, and they know it: Noah, Elijah, Samuel, Marco, Arianna, Grace, Madeline, Simon, and Olivia.

Thanks to Jack and Pat Wilson, and Julie, Mike, and Andrew Vorthman, for sharing your family with Bob and me. Your visits, phone calls, and inquiries about the book lifted my spirits and kept me going.

Most of all I thank my husband and best friend, Bob Laman, bread maker, wood worker, photographer, and constant inquirer, whose love for learning is the model I use when teaching others. Thank you for building the garden that I can see from my office window. It reminds me that with good soil, enough water, and sunshine, anything can grow. Bob's steadiness, love for me, and our shared life and conversations sustain me. I am grateful that I get a lifetime to know and love this remarkable human being.

Introduction
Seeing Possibilities for Growth in Ourselves and in Our Students

In 1993, in a twelve-year-old Nissan packed with six cardboard boxes, I
steered my way 1,500 miles across the country, from Ohio to New Mexico,
toward the Navajo reservation where I was going to teach. I arrived in Gallup,
New Mexico, my new home, on New Year's Eve and checked into the El Ran-
cho hotel. The lobby had wood paneling, a large stone fireplace, and a double
stairwell with ponderosa pine railings. Navajo blankets lay on the backs of
chairs and across the second-story banister. Since the 1940's, movie stars like
John Wayne, Katherine Hepburn, Spencer Tracy, and Gregory Peck had
stayed at this hotel when filming movies in the Four Corners region. Black-
and-white signed photographs of these actors hung on the walls, all suggesting
the hotel's more elegant past.

I heard people speaking Navajo for the first time, its clipped cadence unlike any language I had heard before. That night I stood on the balcony outside my hotel room and felt small, looking out into a night replete with stars
so different from the hazy skies of my metropolitan upbringing. For the first
time, I could see the edge of town where the lights ended and total darkness
began. I felt far from everything and everyone I had ever known.

On Monday morning, I visited my classroom. When I arrived at the
school, my new principal promptly took me to my classroom—a revamped
storage room—and introduced me to my students. The children greeted me,
"Yah-ta-hey" (*Hello*). My students predominantly spoke Navajo. I did not. My
five years of undergraduate study and teacher preparation brought me to this
moment, and now I had no idea what to do or how I could possibly communicate with children who did not yet speak English.

I struggled that first year to understand how most of my students did not have running water or electricity, how they lived along dirt roads that became treacherous and impassable when there was snow or rain causing students to miss school—sometimes for a week at a time, or how some children could live in dorms at the school, so far from their families. That year, I learned to speak enough Navajo to maintain some semblance of control so I could keep my job, but I never learned enough to communicate thoughtfully with parents and community members. I was working hard, and I wanted to be a good teacher. I wanted my students to love learning to read and write, but I couldn't understand what prevented my students from learning—other than the fact that they did not speak English or spoke very limited English. So I blamed my students, their families, and their culture. That year, I found myself thinking (and sometimes even saying) things like:

1. In order to learn English, children must be immersed in English-only environments.

2. If I let the children speak their own language, then I don't know what they are talking about.

3. These children are not invested in being literate in their first or second language.

Looking back, I know these opinions and misunderstandings about language learning were uninformed and prevented me from being the best teacher for those five- and six-year-olds. Ultimately, these beliefs excused me from offering the best education to my students.

Luckily, I had teaching colleagues who were patient with me. Joan, my teaching assistant, who was Navajo, talked to me each day after school and told me how I misunderstood things my students said or did. One day, I asked the children where my scissors were. Jake looked at me and pursed his lips together like he was kissing the air. Then other children did the same thing. I had no idea what this kissing motion meant or why Jake didn't answer me. I thought the children were being rude, until Joan told me that pursing one's lips indicated direction and location because using one's fingers was considered rude. I also learned that holding hands was taboo, so all of the hand-holding songs I learned as an undergraduate had to be modified. Daily events like these continually reminded me of my own unexamined cultural beliefs and practices.

Joan had been forced to attend a boarding school run by the Bureau of Indian Affairs, far from her family and community. She told me about being beaten for speaking Navajo and having her hair cut, the ultimate humiliation for a Navajo child. She invited me to see her group that performed traditional Navajo dances and recommended books for me to read so that I could begin to understand and learn about the unique culture in which I was teaching.

In addition to trying to become more sensitive to my students' cultural practices, I also had to address the academic challenges that some of the students faced. The Reading Recovery teacher told me that by second grade, some of our students were already one year behind. I knew that if I was going to be an effective teacher of Navajo children, I had to learn more so I could support my students in all aspects of their lives.

To do this, I read professional literature that colleagues had given me so I could learn more about language and literacy learning. This reading, in conjunction with conversations with my coworkers, helped me see the rich language and cultural resources my students carried with them each day. I began to document my observations of the children in order to understand what they did know. I discovered that my kindergarten students loved imaginary play. On the playground, they would turn small rocks into cars and build make-believe racetracks in the dirt. They loved reenacting stories I read to them. They also often sang songs when swinging, and so Joan and I recorded their songs and made charts with the words for shared-reading time. By the end of the year, I felt like I finally was getting some things right.

Shifting Perspective and Pedagogy

Two years later, I got to teach my former kindergartners when they entered third grade. While I couldn't take away the mistakes I made as their kindergarten teacher, I worked hard to be a better teacher by building on the following practices, which supported my students' first-language resources:

1. Integrating Navajo into my instruction

2. Having Joan help me translate during whole-group teaching and conferences

3. Reserving daily instructional time for Navajo language instruction

4. Guiding class inquiries into Navajo language, history, and culture

5. Teaching explicit literacy strategies that helped students monitor their own reading and writing in English

6. Incorporating literature that related to my students' lives

7. Inviting community experts to the classroom to teach about important contributions Navajos have made in our cultural, political, and professional lives

8. Shifting away from writing prompts and toward writing for more authentic purposes

I wasn't a perfect teacher that year (I'm still not), but I became more informed. I implemented many of the practices above within a writing workshop framework (Graves 1983). My students wrote narratives about shearing sheep, visiting the medicine man when they were sick, going to the hospital to see their grandparents. They wrote Navajo alphabet books for the kindergarten classes, recorded interviews with elders in the community, then wrote short biographies of the elders' lives, wrote a class newsletter, and wrote nonfiction pieces. Twenty years later, I still have some of that student work because those children taught me lessons that I carry with me each time I begin work with new children, teachers, and schools.

I share my experiences with my Navajo students because, as educators, we have to acknowledge our limited experiences so we can open ourselves to learning more. I was like most teachers in the United States, 83% of whom are White, monolingual, and middle class (National Center for Education Statistics, http://nces.ed.gov). I was also part of the 90–97 percent of teachers who did not receive any training in working with English language learners (National Center for Education Statistics, http://nces.ed.gov).

We must challenge ourselves to have high expectations for ourselves as both learners and teachers when we walk into a classroom with diverse needs. My experience reminded me that each new place I worked—from Belize as a Peace Corps volunteer to Indiana as a substitute teacher and doctoral student, to South Carolina as a professor—required that I come to know my students as individuals. It required me to work to identify and document the resources that children bring with them to school. Through strong teaching, multilingual students can expand their range of literacy practices. And we, their teachers, can also grow and change as we get to know our students as individuals with talents, strengths, interests, and concerns, because we no longer expect them to conform to us or to curriculum that is irrelevant.

The Languages We Speak Matter

Language is inextricably linked to our identities, not only as learners but also as human beings (Carey 2007; Nieto 2010). When children come to our classrooms, they have grown up in families and communities where they have already learned a lot about language and the nuances of communicating. I've learned that what children know when they come to school is fertile ground for learning and cultivating a relevant curriculum (Allen 2010; Freeman and Freeman 2007). My Navajo students knew things that I did not know. They knew how to herd sheep, tell creation stories, sing traditional songs, keep a fire going, speak Navajo, use traditional herbs for healing, and so much more. Denying someone the language(s) with which they first learned to make meaning of their world is to deny them a significant part of what makes them who they are, as well as prevents them from using what they know in order to learn. This is true not only for students who come to school speaking other languages and language varieties than those of their teachers. It is part of our human experience. We each develop an ear for the language communities where we grew up. We are attuned to these regional and cultural ways with words, and we have biases toward them.

The Shifting Demographics of Our Classrooms

English language learners are not new to U.S. schools, but this population continues to become more diverse. Children who are considered English language learners may have recently immigrated to the United States, been born in the

United States, be refugees from war-torn areas, live in relative economic comfort or be economically vulnerable (Salomone 2010). English language learners may speak more than one language. Some may speak some English, while others are newcomers to English. Some may have had extensive educational experience and be literate in the languages they speak, while others may have had limited or no previous schooling (Suárez-Orozco, Suárez-Orozco, and Todorova 2008). Because of these varied backgrounds and contexts, we need to make intentional efforts to get to know our students in order to address their individual instructional needs and understand their experiences.

States like California, Texas, Arizona, Florida, New York, and New Mexico (where I was living and working) have a long history of educating large populations of children who speak languages other than English (Edelsky, Smith, and Faltis 2008). However, in the past thirty years demographics have shifted, and the percentage of English language learners has increased significantly. Between 1980 and 2009, the number of school-age children speaking languages other than English at home rose from 4.7 to 11.2 million (National Center for Education Statistics, Indicator 6). More to the point, children in U.S. schools speak more than 350 different languages, with approximately 77 percent of those students speaking Spanish (National Center for Education Statistics). And today English language learners are enrolled in schools across the country in "new growth states" like North Carolina, Indiana, Georgia, Alabama, and South Carolina, where educators are confronting the challenges of educating larger ELL populations than ever before (National Center for Education Statistics, Indicator 8).

Sadly, we are not meeting the needs of this growing multilingual population. Nationally, English language learners have a fifty percent drop-out rate, twice the national average (Espinosa, 2008). With one in five children in the United States now speaking languages other than English at home and in their communities (National Center for Education Statistics), and with most teachers having little or no professional development in supporting English language learners, we have a lot of work to do in order to avoid failing more students.

Possibilities Instead of Problems

When we turn on the radio on any given day, we hear about the "global economy." While English is a significant part of the global economy, so are many other languages, including Chinese, German, French, Japanese, Vietnamese, and Spanish. We live in a time where speaking multiple languages is an asset. As a result, Danling Fu points out in her book *Writing Between Languages*, multilingual children are at the leading edge of the global economy (Fu 2009). She further notes that even though acquiring language is a complex cognitive process, over half of the world's population speaks more than one language. This implies that children are certainly capable of learning more than one language.

Researchers like Luis Moll, Sonia Nieto, Kris Gutiérrez, and others help educators move from seeing educating ELLs as a *problem* to be solved and instead as a *possibility* to be engaged. They remind us that ELLs have tremendous linguistic and cultural resources, coping mechanisms, and resilience that can support these students in academic contexts (Suárez-Orozco, Suárez-Orozco, and Todorova 2008). For instance, English language learners come to classrooms already speaking a language, such as Spanish. They have done what all children do when they start school: learned a language. Gutiérrez and Orellana (2006) urge researchers and educators to reframe conversations about English language learners that position ELLs as problems:

> . . . we might ask how well schools and classrooms adapt to the presence of students from non-dominant groups, or how schools and classrooms can be transformed to better serve these students. This shifts the onus for adaptation from students to the institution. Or we can push the question further, by asking not how people change to fit their context or how contexts change to fit people but rather how change occurs both in the participants and the contexts of their participation. (119)

Too often English language learners are expected to adapt to dominant ways of teaching and learning (for example, teachers asking questions and children providing short answers). English language learners read and study academic content that often does not mention contributions from cultures or people from outside the United States or from a variety of ethnic backgrounds (Nieto 2010). Holidays like Christmas are celebrated with a disregard that so many cultures do not celebrate Christian holidays (Nieto 2010). When we learn *with* and *from* our students, we have opportunities to build on students' strengths through talk, shared inquiries, and a curriculum that is relevant to their lives. I am drawn to the idea that all human relationships have the capacity and potential to change who we are and inform our teaching.

It is because of that belief that I have committed my teaching career to developing multilingual students' potential. I am both optimistic and realistic when it comes to teaching English language learners; we have a lot of work to do. We know that it takes five to seven years, and sometimes longer, for English language learners to acquire academic English—the vocabulary associated with school-related content (August and Shanahan 2006; Cummins 1996). This means we need to provide excellent instruction within meaningful learning contexts, where we are continually monitoring multilingual children's learning and supporting their academic development.

How This Book Can Help

All of this data means we have to teach writing *while* children are learning to speak, read, and write in English. We cannot wait until children reach a certain level of English proficiency before we introduce them to writing, and we cannot teach writing under the guise of fill-in-the-blank worksheets or other narrow language exercises that are frequently used with English language learners (Fu 2009; Rueda, August, and Goldenberg 2006; Samway 2005). When multilingual children engage in writing projects that are personally relevant, build on their background knowledge, use their home languages, and require them to write for authentic reasons, ELLs become more engaged in writing and develop understandings about writing processes and practices (Freeman and Freeman 2001; Fu 2009; Samway 2006).

This book will give you insight and practical tips to engage multilingual students in a writing workshop process. Specifically, I'll offer my experience and advice in the following areas:

1. Setting up a writing workshop that engages all levels of multilingual learners (Chapter 1)

2. Building community through shared language practices and adapting focused mini-lessons for multilingual students (Chapters 2 and 3)

3. Scaffolding independent practice for a wide variety of multilingual learners (Chapter 4)

4. Tailoring conferences to support multilingual writers during independent writing time (Chapter 5)

5. Facilitating and encouraging multilingual students to share and reflect (Chapters 6 and 7)

As you read each chapter, you'll find specific tools and strategies that will help make your writing instruction meet the needs of multilingual writers. You'll also find students' writing samples with explanations of the significance of the multilingual writer's work. Each chapter ends with classroom and student observations and/or planning notes, based on the information in that chapter. My goal is for you to see how each idea presented in this book can become part of a cumulative story of instruction, as well as the true step-by-step story of how we become better as teachers.

Writing Workshop

A Framework for Multilingual Writers

It's writing time in Susan Ross' second-grade classroom. Children are at their desks or on the carpet. Some are standing and some are sitting. Some are working in pairs, and others are alone, huddled near the bookshelves. As always, there is lots of talk: nothing too distracting, just enough to remind me that this classroom is filled with young people who have plenty on their minds, especially when they are hard at work.

I visit this classroom regularly during writing time. Today, I grab my notepad, recorder, and pen and join a group of five children who are at a table working in their writer's notebooks. David asks Noor, "What's that?" He points to the Hindi characters she has written in her notebook. "That's Hindi," Noor says with a matter-of-fact tone and then shows David how to write her name in Hindi. Next to her, Akira, a new student from Japan, is writing entries in her writer's notebook for her *All About* book in Japanese, just below her detailed illustrations of a Buddhist temple. Next to Akira are two students, Eduardo and Leon, both from Mexico, who are speaking Spanish to one another while they compose in English. David, a monolingual English-speaking student, looks at me and says, "Sheesh! I gotta learn *another* language!"

Susan's classroom looks so different than my first classroom did. In Susan's room, children are not discouraged from speaking or writing in their first languages because Susan understands the role that children's languages play in their literacy development. Susan and her students create a multilingual community—a community much like in the real world—where people speak, think, write, and read languages other than English. For all intents and purposes, Susan is monolingual. She remembers a bit of French and Spanish from high school, which she finds useful every now and then, but she would never claim to be bilingual. But, unlike many classrooms in the United States, students in Susan's classroom are encouraged to use their first language(s) as a way to communicate with one another and as a tool for making meaning. Susan says with deep conviction, "I don't want them to forget how to speak their home language(s). They can learn English without giving up their language(s)." What Susan understands is that in order to learn anything new, humans need to feel valued and recognized for who they are. And the language(s) students speak are an integral part of their identity, as well as an important resource for learning. As classrooms in the United States become rich with students who speak multiple languages, we have opportunities to build classroom communities like Susan's, where we welcome multilingual children as capable and competent learners. Writing workshop offers a curricular structure where multilingual children are able to be and become writers.

Rethinking Labels: Shifting from English Language Learner to Multilingual Learner

In the title of this book and in the introduction, I use the term *English language learner*, or *ELLs*, because it is frequently used and most educators are familiar with it, but from here on, I use the term *multilingual* to identify children who come to classrooms speaking languages other than English. How we label things matters because it shapes our perceptions and even our actions (Langer 1989), and in taking up Gutiérrez's and Orellana's (2006) challenge to reframe how we talk about English language learners, I use the term *multilingual* in this book because it emphasizes students' languages and their literacies as an important learning resource (Cummins 2006). Though *English language learner* is prevalent in educational parlance—and is an improvement over the term *Limited English Proficient* (LEP), which was used in educational policy and research for years—it still seems to define children's only job as learning English instead of also learning science, math, reading, and writing. *Multilingual* describes students by what they have versus what they lack (English). Although students who are coming to our classrooms may not yet be multilingual, it's a goal worth aspiring to: that children do not have to give up the language(s) they already know in order to learn English, but instead are supported as they acquire new languages. There is overwhelming evidence that being multilingual has cognitive benefits that support learning English (Cummins 2006; August and Shanahan 2006; Freeman and Freeman 2006; Fu 2009).

A Note About Language Learning

Multilingual students have ranges of experience in learning English. Throughout the book, I try to give a sense of where students are in their English language learning by drawing on descriptions from the TESOL standards (see complete descriptions at www.tesol.org). These standards include the word *levels*, but I don't use that word. As Ms. Rodriguez, a kindergarten teacher said, "When I look at students I don't see levels, I just see what they are currently doing and that guides my teaching." However, the TESOL descriptors may be helpful for understanding students' current English language learning and to see their writing production in relationship to that. I have also revised some of the descriptors to indicate what students are doing rather than what they are not yet doing.

Starting (newcomers)—Speak language(s) other than English for communication. They respond to simple commands, statements, and questions. May use single words and simple phrases

Emerging—Understands phrases and short sentences; uses memorized phrases, groups of words, and formulae; and uses simple structures. Begins to use general academic vocabulary and everyday expressions

Developing—Produces more complex speech and still requires some repetition. Uses English spontaneously but may still have difficulty expressing all of their thoughts since they are still learning vocabulary and more complex language structures

Expanding—Communicates in English in new and unfamiliar settings. Learning academic language in context is important for supporting continued language learning

Bridging—Can express themselves fluently and spontaneously on a wide range of personal, general, and academic topics. Can function with English-dominant speakers and has a command of academic vocabulary, idiomatic expressions, and colloquialisms

Why Use Writing Workshop for Multilingual Writers?

Over the past thirty years, research and accounts of teaching writing in and through writing workshop as a curricular structure has informed much of what we know about writing instruction and how children come to understand writing as a process and practice (Anderson 2000; Bomer 1995, 2010; Calkins 1998; Graves 1983; Wood Ray 1999, 2001). In writing workshops, children learn to write by studying the work of writers: how writers choose topics, how they develop a piece of writing from gathering ideas to publication, by learning strategies for drafting their writing, by revising and attending to editing, by learning to read like a writer, and finally by publishing their writing for authentic audiences.

Much of this previous research focused on students who speak English as a first language, with some mention and examples from English language learners (Samway 2006). But unlike their monolingual peers, multilingual children face unique challenges when learning to write in English. Multilingual children have to develop understandings about English grammatical structure (such as subject/verb/object in sentences), more and less formal styles of writing dependent upon purpose and audience (genre), and punctuation, to name a few (Gibbons 2002; Schatz and Wilkinson 2012). Multilingual children may even have to learn concepts of print regarding kinds of scripts, such as Chin-Hwa, a Chinese-speaking student, who had to learn to write using the English alphabet. Latin script is very different from the logographic symbols of Chinese (Schatz and Wilkinson 2012). In addition, Chin-Hwa had to learn to write from left to right instead of from right to left. These are not challenges that English-speaking children, especially older students, face. And so we take these issues into consideration as we design a writing workshop that supports multilingual students who are learning to write in English.

Writing workshop has been criticized in regards to teaching multilingual children and children who speak dialects of English and who are not from middle-class English-speaking backgrounds (Delpit 1988; Gibbons 2002). Some argue that students cannot learn to write simply by giving them paper and pencil and encouraging them to write every day because multilingual children need explicit instruction in text features, language structures, and academic discourses (Gibbons 2002). But immersion in writing workshop does not mean "sink or swim" for multilingual students. No one learns without support, practice, guidance, and feedback, and writing workshop provides multilingual students the space and time to practice what they are learning. It also gives their teachers the time to pay close attention to that learning in order to guide their current and future instruction. Learning to write in a second or third language is a complex undertaking, but it is not impossible. Indeed, it is essential if we are going to foster multilingual children's sense of identity and agency.

In fact, there are studies of multilingual students and writing workshop that shine a light on the possibilities and potential of adapting instruction within writing workshop to support English language learners (Buly 2011; Freeman and Freeman 2001; Hudelson 1984; Laman and Van Sluys 2008; Samway 2005; Van Sluys 2003). You don't have to consider yourself a writing workshop teacher to use the invitations and strategies in this book. Many of the strategies can be adapted so that you can try out these teaching techniques without making large-scale change. My hope is that these strategies will make an argument for using writing workshop as the key curricular structure for teaching writing to multilingual students. But I also use the writing workshop structure because it changed my teaching for the better and because of the difference it has made for many teachers I have worked with over the years who teach multilingual children.

What Is Writing Workshop?

In my work as a classroom teacher, teacher educator, and staff developer, I have seen many instructional practices that are described as "Writing process" or "Writing workshop." Some writing process classrooms have a classroom chart that contains a vertical bulleted list with words such as "select topic, draft, revise, edit, and publish." Sometimes students are given a topic to write about and are then told to move through each of the steps one at a time so that every week they have a completed product. While each of these actions is part of the writing process, writers are quick to point out that writing does not follow a step-by-step process.

Instead, I find Randy Bomer's (1995) model of the writing process more helpful (see Figure 1.1) because it is a recursive process: writers generate ideas for writing projects by first living a life, then they begin collecting ideas in a writer's notebook (though we don't do this with our youngest writers), then they spend time nurturing ideas by writing in more depth or from a different angle, conducting research,

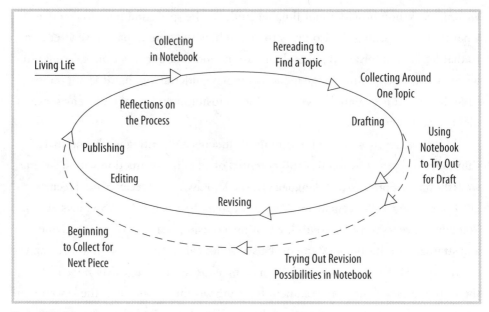

Reflections on
the Process

Collecting
in Notebook

Rereading to
Find a Topic

Living Life

Collecting Around
One Topic

Drafting

Using
Notebook
to Try Out
for Draft

Publishing

Editing

Revising

Beginning
to Collect for
Next Piece

Trying Out Revision
Possibilities in Notebook

Figure 1.1

and then moving out of the notebook to a draft, then revising and editing until the writing is ready for publication. This process often moves back and forth between these practices. For example, even though my current writing project is this book, I continue to write in my writer's notebook about my childhood as I gather ideas for a memoir for my mother. These practices don't happen in a lockstep fashion: living a life and collecting ideas on Monday, nurturing a seed idea on Tuesday, drafting on Wednesday, revising on Thursday, and editing and publishing on Friday. Instead, a writing project may last from one to six weeks, depending on children's ages and the particular project.

The way we spend time in the writing workshop with multilingual students is no different from how we spend time with monolingual students. These structures have been articulated in many resources about writing workshop (Bomer 1995; Calkins 1994; Wood Ray 2001). The structures of writing workshop work best when they reflect what we currently know and understand about effective instruction for multilingual students.

Guidelines for Writing Workshop Structure

Every writing workshop typically includes the following structure:

1. **Minilesson** This 5–10 minute lesson is used to teach content about writing processes (collecting, nurturing, drafting, revising, editing, publishing), or about craft (genre lessons, reading like writers, beginnings, etc.), or something that you notice many of your students need help with (final punctuation). In the multilingual classroom, there will also be some minilessons that pertain to language instruction.

2. **Independent Writing Time** This 20–45 minute block of time is the majority of the writing workshop time when children are working on their independent writing. Students understand that each day they return to the previous day's work and continue with their writing projects. Even though the work is independent, it is not individual. Children often talk with one another during this time. Teachers circulate around the room and conduct writing conferences with individual students.

3. **Sharing Time** The last 5–10 minutes of every workshop is time for students to share what they have learned that day as writers, to highlight a particularly informative writing conference, or to share a portion of their writing. This last part of the workshop reminds students that thinking about their writing work is essential and that there are others who are interested in their writing.

How Does the Structure of Writing Workshop Help Multilingual Learners?

Writing workshop can help a wide range of students. These principles make it particularly useful for multilingual learners:

- Writing workshop has a consistent structure and routine, using familiar language

- It is highly contextualized (students are learning about writing while engaged in writing for authentic reasons)

- It provides whole-group (very short and direct), small-group, and individual instruction, where students have access to grade-level curriculum and instruction tailored to their academic needs

- It builds on students' strengths by asking them to write what they know in the language(s) they know

- It provides opportunities for authentic English language instruction within the context of students' writing

- It allows students to speak the language(s) they know and to speak with native English speakers in authentic contexts

- It generates curriculum from what teachers learn about their students in this process

- It helps students develop agency by learning to make the kinds of decisions that authors must make

The difference in a writing workshop with multilingual students is that in each part of the writing workshop we have to pay more attention to how we convey content for multilingual students. We provide visual cues as well as verbal instructions in order to build students' overall literacy skills. We may use props that we wouldn't normally use with monolingual English-speaking children. We use books written in languages other than English as model texts. Throughout this book, I highlight specific ways to support multilingual students in the writing workshop. I believe these adaptations are not only effective but are essential for students' success in learning English. In building these everyday practices, we also build community and rituals that lay the foundation for building a thriving writing workshop.

2

Knowing and Being Known

A few years ago, I read Barbara Kingsolver's *Animal, Vegetable, Miracle: A Year of Food Life* (2007) and became obsessed with facts and statistics about food production and consumption. I found myself reading labels in the produce aisle to see just how far my bananas and mangos had traveled. Kingsolver claims that within one generation, Americans have lost their knowledge of and connection to food production. She also reports that in the history of humankind, we have eaten from among eighty thousand plant species and now most of us eat from among just eight (49). I was alarmed, suddenly aware of what could happen to food availability and sustainability if certain species are destroyed.

That summer I visited my eighty-six-year-old grandmother and talked with her about the book and Kingsolver's decision to move her family to Virginia, where they raised their own food for a year. Our conversation revealed rich stories of her daily life on the farm that I had not known until then. She remembered canning food from their garden as a young girl. In the winter months, her father would hang a side of beef outside because the meat would stay frozen, and he would cut off what they needed for meals. She had to step through deep snow as she carried a lantern to light her way to the dairy barn and the cows waiting inside for their daily milking. Much of her family's time was spent growing, preserving, and preparing food.

My conversation with my grandmother reminded me that if I can know someone my entire life and still not know everything about them then an essential first step toward building community is being willing to listen to other people's stories. To take risks, to grow as learners, students must feel that they are known and that they know one another, including their teacher. Every school day, first to last, we need to demonstrate our curiosity about who our students are. By modeling that curiosity, we encourage them to recognize that they are interesting and that other people are interesting; we invite them to engage with the world and with one another.

The beginning of the school year is typically sprinkled with getting-to-know-you activities—interest surveys, summer vacation stories, hobby posters, etc.—but these activities mean little unless they trigger deeper conversations and create real human connections. We sometimes forget that the foundation of our curriculum is children's lives. If we don't value and recognize their lives and acknowledge their experiences, then any instruction we provide is a house without a foundation, unstable and impermanent. The diverse cultures and languages of our students are an invitation to learn about the world and ourselves. Through exploration, we affirm diversity (Nieto 2010), build learning communities that value home languages (as well as English), and remind all students of the value of examination and reflection.

No matter what mandates come down the curricular pike, we must remember that our students are individuals; they are composed of more than one aspect. They love cartoons, have rock collections, fight with their siblings, help their fathers paint windows, are sometimes frightened and sometimes brave; they are kids who want us to like them and to find them interesting. Supporting our students as learners by first recognizing who they are is the most important work we can do when creating a meaningful curriculum.

Reclaiming the Word "Community"

In educational circles, the word *community* is thrown around (and away) a lot (Wenger 1998). I've heard a controlled classroom—one in which the students are always quiet—described as "a great classroom community." I've also heard a classroom in which everyone is always happy, untroubled by difficult subjects or conversations, called "a great classroom community." I would like to reclaim the notion of "classroom community" as a place where we, alongside our students, develop ways of talking, thinking, interacting, and valuing one another as human beings, where things are not always easy, but they *are* dynamic, engaging, and respectful. At its best, a classroom community is a place where students get to be and become distinct individuals and grow into the identities they want to create for themselves. Identity should never be a superficial element to learning; as Wenger explains, it is the vehicle for learning:

> As a trajectory, an identity must incorporate a past and a future. Learning communities will become places of identity to the extent they make trajectories possible—that is, to the extent they offer a past and a future that can be experienced as a personal trajectory. (215)

This concept is especially true for multilingual students, whose experiences are sometimes quite different from our own. Multilingual children need to know that they do not have to give up who they are or the languages they speak in order to develop their literacies. We have the opportunity to learn with and from multilingual students about the languages they speak, their interests, and their cultural and linguistic resources, while supporting their learning in and through English. By modeling new learning ourselves, we can create a thriving writing workshop, one that makes all of our students more conscious and curious about language, identity, and culture.

A Hawk's-Eye View of Your Classroom Environment

To foster this environment, we need to see both the big picture, such as our students' growth as writers over the course of a year, as well as the tiniest of daily details, such as whether the chart by the door effectively communicates yesterday's teaching point. Like a hawk that sees both the cornfield and the tail of a mouse from hundreds of feet above, we move our attention back and forth to see how each small detail reflects the big-picture beliefs we have about a writing community. Because our classroom is a familiar place, usually one we return to every year and set up in more or less the same way, the small details can become invisible to us, and, if asked, we might find ourselves struggling to explain how some of the details reflect our beliefs. One of the best ways to start this process is to look at your classroom environment with fresh eyes and ask yourself some basic questions.

Questions to Ask Yourself . . .
About Your Classroom Environment

Each bolded statement below communicates a belief that is essential to building a writing community. It is followed by a question you can pose to evaluate whether your classroom environment communicates that belief.

- **We are a community of writers.** Is there a meeting area where everyone can sit together to learn new strategies for writing and to read their work aloud? (You'll find more on building community through whole-group instruction in Chapter 3 and on sharing and publishing work in Chapter 6.)

- **Writers often work independently but sometimes collaborate to get someone else's expertise.** Are there spaces set up, such as tables, desks, or comfortable floor areas, that allow students to work independently but that also support collaboration when appropriate? (You'll find more on independent and partner work in Chapter 4 and on writing conferences in Chapter 5.)

- **Writers read.** Is there a classroom library with space for children to display the texts they love, texts that inspire their own writing? (For details on building a multilingual, multicultural classroom library, see page 25.)

- **All writers publish.** Is there a place where published student work is displayed? Does the published work posted reflect all of the students in the class on a regular basis? (You'll find more on publishing in Chapter 6.)

- **All writers follow a process and use tools of the craft.** Are there charts that support independent student work by providing important reminders about the writing process and craft? Is there a writing tools station, stocked with staplers, dual-language dictionaries, paper, word walls with common sight words as well as words your students frequently use, computers for research and word processing, etc., basically everything a writer might need? (You'll find more on supporting the writing process of multilingual students in Chapters 3 and 4.)

> - **Writers are interested in people and the world.** How does this space reflect an interest in multilingual students' lives? (For some specific ideas, see page 15.)
>
> - **As a community of writers, we know that not everyone writes in English and that all languages have value.** What languages do my students speak this year? If I look around my room, can I see all their languages incorporated in some way? (For some specific ideas on incorporating home languages, see page 21.)

Although not all of these questions are specific to multilingual students, they do define our classroom space as supportive of our students as writers—or not. They also remind us that our students are often new to much of what we take for granted. The design of a space not only defines the kind of activity that goes on there but also communicates the value of the people who occupy it. We criticize some spaces for making us feel small or less human. A poorly designed hospital feels overwhelming: every floor looks the same, leaving us uncertain if we're in the right place when we get off the elevator. One could argue that this design helps to reinforce the authority of the nurses and doctors and leads us to relinquish some of our authority as patients. We don't want the same dichotomy of authority in our classrooms, however. Classroom space should reinforce students' agency.

Rows of individual desks discourage talking and collaboration, both of which are essential to community building. This traditional image of a classroom was an intentional reimagining of the factory production line: education as a machine, stamping out identical (student) products. This has also been described as a banking model of education (Freire 2003) in which teachers deposit knowledge and students withdraw (memorize) dates, facts, and formulas. This model was partially created out of fear of the large immigrant populations entering the United States at that time. How quickly could these students be assimilated and made homogeneous, English-speaking only, Americans (Salomone 2010; Suárez-Orozco, Suárez-Orozco, and Todorova 2008)? This model and the rote memorization that defined instruction failed many children and made content inaccessible to students who spoke languages other than English (Nieto 2010; Salomone 2010).

Today we know so much more about how learning happens—it is individual and social, cultural and dynamic—and our classroom environment needs to reflect those understandings. Navigating the classroom environment with confidence and ease is more than a metaphor; students' ownership of their space is synonymous with their ability to learn. When our three-dimensional students show up, we can include them in organizing and arranging the various learning spaces because they are the ones who live, think, and work in these spaces every day. Remember that very few of us have our classroom arrangement set at the beginning of the year, never to be changed, and that there are many variations on effective classroom environment. That said, here's one classroom organization tool that works (see Figure 2.1).

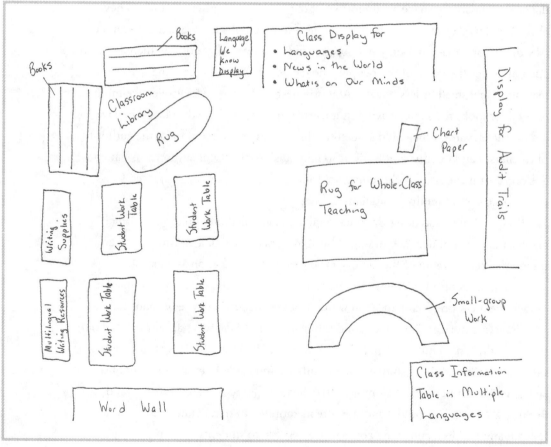

Figure 2.1

Take a Tour of Your Classroom as a Student Would Experience It

I have gone so far as to walk around on my knees in order to see the classroom from my students' perspective. It helps to see if the space makes sense. For example, do children have to walk across the room for writing supplies, or are they centrally located so that children have quick access to the tools they need? As teachers, we do not use the room the way our students do: we are usually taller, we don't always sit on the rug surrounded by other children, and we don't sit at children's desks or tables alongside other children all day. Trying to move around the room the way students do helps us identify (and then address) possible obstacles to learning.

Writers Are Curious about People and the World

The static qualities of physical space are something we can reflect upon and carefully construct, but once our students walk into the space, it becomes dynamic. The teacher is a kind of magical mirror: we reflect back to our students how we want them to be in the world by our own behavior. We want our students to see themselves as writers, and one of the essential traits of a writer is to be curious about people and the world. As soon as students cross the threshold of our classroom, we demonstrate our curiosity about them, which serves as a model for students as we invite them into our writing community by asking them about themselves.

Authentic talk is the most powerful tool we have. Education researchers have helped us understand that talk is *the* teaching tool of our trade (Johnston 2004, 2012; Barnes 1992). Talk is fleeting; we can't fix it in place and examine it the way we can a piece of student writing, yet there is much we can do to cultivate classrooms that value and examine talk. Discussing, arguing, sharing, questioning, explaining, comparing, and exploring are how we make meaning for ourselves and for others. Talk mediates our learning. When classrooms are quiet throughout the day, I worry; it generally means that students are not learning how to think, debate, or participate. This has important consequences for all children, especially those who are multilingual.

As children pass through hallways and doorways, I ask them questions and they tell me stories: "Dr. Laman, my mama had the baby last night. She was three weeks early!" During recess, children flushed from running stop mid-chase to tell me about their birthday party or an upcoming family reunion. I know we are often in a rush to move students from one curricular moment to the next or down the hallway to the cafeteria, but those inconvenient moments are often the ones when children are ready to talk and when we need to model receptivity by attentively listening and asking questions. As we build multilingual learners' confidence in the English language, this time is particularly important.

I also connect children's stories to their writing lives by asking whether they've written about them yet. I may remind them that the story would be a great topic for a poem, a picture book, or a piece of nonfiction they are writing. They don't always follow through, but I've alerted them that the events that make up their days have the potential to be written about. These casual moments might seem insignificant, but it's their informality that makes them authentic, connecting students' lives to what happens in our classroom and its relevance to the curriculum.

Multilingual students may spend the better part of their days speaking languages other than English at home or in their communities and therefore need authentic reasons and opportunities to speak English. If we're not encouraging multilingual students to talk in the classroom and during the school day, we may be excluding them from their education and from opportunities to practice English in meaningful contexts. Too often, multilingual children are present but not talking. Ironically, teachers sometimes allow multilingual children to remain silent because they don't want to embarrass a child who may not yet feel confident speaking English. As teachers, we can feel a little uncomfortable in our first attempts to talk to students who are newcomers to English. But "uncomfortable" isn't the same as "impossible." And it is our job to help multilingual learners grow. Children don't learn how to tell stories, explain their thinking, or disagree with others through silence or isolation. Language learning improves the more meaningful speech is produced in the company of others who care (Freeman and Freeman 2001; Houk 2005; Krashen 1982; Soltero 2011). Here are some suggestions to build confidence in engaging multilingual students in supportive talk.

Initiating Talk with Multilingual Students Who Are Newcomers to English

- Learn a few words or phrases in each multilingual student's language. Initially, these can be general: "How are you?" "Hello," "Goodbye," "Thank you," and "Have a great day!" but what you learn about your student can guide you in acquiring some new language: "I saw you score a goal at recess. Do you play a lot of soccer, Farid?"

- Ask embedded yes/no questions and statements: "Were you mad when that happened? Here's what we can do to make that go better . . ." "Did you go to your grandma's house this weekend?"; "Is that your sister?"

- Extend students' talk by asking them questions or encouraging them to tell you more: "That's interesting! Tell me more about it," "Then what happened?" "Why?"

- Name what the child does at appropriate, positive moments to demonstrate the words for the child's actions: "Maricar, great job getting the writing supplies you needed quickly and quietly!"

- Name what the child does in her writing and her work: "Oh, you made a house and added words to your story!"

- Be prepared to talk more than the child, but keep creating opportunities for the child to talk with you and others.

- Remember that some students may be very quiet or may not talk at all. Be sensitive to this; create opportunities but don't pressure children. Document your observations when students do talk. For example, do they speak with peers who share the same language(s)? How do they communicate with English-dominant peers? Use these observations to help inform your talk with children and the kinds of teaching contexts you create.

Morning Meeting: Learning to Be Curious About Each Other

If we want to build a community of multilingual writers, we need to create opportunities throughout the day for children to tell stories—to compose and structure events in ways that communicate details, change, and significance. Morning meeting is a daily event in which all members of our classroom community can become storytellers: "Tell us about a time you were surprised." "Tell us about something you had never heard of before." "Tell us about your first memory." "Tell us about your morning so far." If multilingual students give very brief answers, I usually say, "Tell us more." That phrase seems too simple to be effective, but if we pay attention, we may be surprised by how often we let multilingual students give us one-word answers.

When we ask students to tell us more, we encourage them to elaborate in meaningful ways and show them that there is significance in the details of their lives. For students who are learning English, telling more builds vocabulary, expands their sentence length and structure, and stretches their ability to convey meaning. As teachers, we can scaffold this talk. As children add more, we can supply words they may need, repeat what they said, or ask questions that we know students can answer. However, these prompts aren't appropriate for complete newcomers to English;

we may need to ask these students some yes/no questions such as, "Did you see pumpkins during the field trip yesterday?" Or we can ask a question in the student's language, or give children objects to refer to, such as photos, toys, puppets, or drawings, which provide a concrete reference for children when sharing. We never want to force children to talk (not that we really can); we just want to continually invite and encourage children to talk in multiple languages.

Primary language partners and small groups are important ways to increase multilingual students' opportunities to explain their thinking, negotiate meaning, and extend time engaged in meaningful talk. Smaller settings are also often less intimidating for students. We need to look for these scaffolds that invite multilingual children into the conversation.

On the hundredth day of school in Susan's second-grade classroom, Noor, a girl from India, brought in a poster with one hundred things from India taped to it. There were spices, a *bindi* (a small decoration worn on the forehead), money, candy, flyers, and more. Noor was so eager to share that Susan turned the morning meeting over to her. Noor's talk inspired another student, Harsha, who until that point had not been comfortable sharing with the class, to tell her classmates about traveling to India every summer to visit her extended family. The entire class benefited from the information these two girls provided about the different religions, languages, and experiences of India they each had. Noor's poster hung in the classroom for the rest of the year and was an ongoing resource when children asked Noor and Harsha to tell them more about India.

Decreasing Multilingual Students' Anxiety About Sharing

- Give children a chance to think ahead of time about a story they want to tell. You may write on the board so that students can refer to it. Model your own storytelling. Set students up for success by letting them know that tomorrow you are going to ask them to share a story; this gives them time to practice the story with you or with a family member. For example, "What do you want us to know about you?"

- Give students time to rehearse before sharing with the whole group. Ask them to tell their story to you or a friend first. Very often children can produce more language with a partner than on their own (Gibbons 2002).

- Let students sketch their story before sharing it. Students can refer to the drawing while sharing, and the drawing may help other students better understand the story.

- Have students share in their first language as you, another adult, or another student translates. (Some teachers let children share in their first language even when no one else in the room is able to translate.)

- Ask partners and small groups to share a class experience with the whole group. For example, after going on a walk to examine leaves, have children share what they learned about leaves.

- Encourage pairs of children to share a story with the class.

- Remember that wait time matters. Give multilingual students time to respond.

You can also encourage students to share in morning meeting by trying one of these strategies.

Ask Students to Bring in a Significant Object from Home

Give students the opportunity to teach one another about their languages, cultures, and everyday lives. Variations of this are limitless: students could bring in a significant object one day and share autobiographical collages another. Children, especially those new to speaking English, may find being asked to share stories from their lives intimidating, which is understandable. Over time they will become more comfortable talking in a variety of settings, including in front of the whole class.

It is important that we model listening for all students and that we are particularly patient when multilingual students are speaking. Nodding, asking questions, repeating what children say, and sitting close to multilingual children while they share in case we need to repeat aloud what they may say quietly.

Invite Children's Family and Community Members to Teach the Class Songs or Poems in Children's Languages

This offers further demonstration that multilingualism is common and that children's languages matter and are worth learning. English-dominant children learn words and phrases, poems, and songs in a new language, and students who speak the languages being taught feel more welcome and valuable in the classroom and—most importantly—become experts.

Teachers who try this report that they and their students have significant conversations about which words the children understand, about how the sounds of languages compare, and about what it feels like not to understand every word. (For a list of multicultural and multilingual poems and songs, see Appendix A.)

Not Everyone Writes in English and All Languages Have Value

As the world and our classrooms become more multilingual, it is important to ask ourselves if the texts in our classrooms—including environmental print, books, magazines, music, video—reflect the languages that our students and their families speak. These language-rich resources help us create opportunities to read, discuss, and write about languages and the global community we live in. In order to foster and facilitate a writing curriculum that supports students' multilingual literacies, including but not limited to English, we have to take a close look at what languages are represented in our classrooms and our schools to ensure we explicitly send the message that all languages matter.

Integrate First Languages Using Labels

When you integrate first languages using labels in your classroom environment, you help all students literally see that they are part of this global community. In addition to communicating this important belief, you are supporting your multilingual writers' vocabulary expansion. Labeling helps multilingual students make literacy connections between the languages they speak and English (Freeman and Freeman 2001). Labels also help English-dominant children learn other languages. Multilingual labels and environmental print are a visual affirmation that people read and write in many languages, and that the languages children know are integral to their literate lives and have a place in school.

Incorporating First-Language Labels

- When teaching kindergarten and first grade, or when working with emergent multilingual children at any grade level, the visual cue of an object in the room—and pictures of objects not in the room—next to a written label is very helpful. For example, putting photos next to your daily schedule, such as a photo of food next to the word *lunch* and a photo of children playing next to the word *recess* provides a visual reference for students.

- Create charts boasting: "The languages we know" with words in students' languages and in English. Keep adding to the chart throughout the year.

- In a classroom in which fifteen languages are represented, it is not feasible to include each language on every label, but you can ensure that all labels in the room contain examples from all of the languages the students speak. Make a quick chart to confirm inclusive language representation in the room.

- After taking students on a tour of the school and/or classroom, you can ask them what labels they would find most helpful and invite them to label key areas and items in their native language. If students do not know how to write in their primary language(s), enlist the help of community members, parents, school personnel, the Internet, or bilingual dictionaries. These labels serve an additional purpose for community members who may not speak English and need assistance locating the school office, the lunchroom, or the auditorium.

You can refer to these labels early in the school year as students become accustomed to the classroom. Particularly in the early grades, you may have the whole class practice saying the words on these labels and refer to them when modeling writing, so children come to see that speaking, reading, and writing a number of languages is a valued literacy practice. In Sydney Brice's first-through-third-grade classroom, Adi, a Hebrew-speaker, posted the Hebrew alphabet in the classroom as a reference. She would write in Hebrew and then translate it into English (Laman 2004). Children in the room who did not speak Hebrew often referred to the chart and asked Adi how to write in Hebrew. Demonstrating that your classroom is a place in which everyone is a novice at learning something also has value. In the upper grades, these labels are a resource for comparing languages and learning new languages. See Figure 2.2 for some examples of labeling.

Share Family Members' First-Language Experiences

We continually need to find ways to make schools hospitable to multilingual families. It's important to reassure parents who may be nervous because they are not fluent in English that they are providing a valuable experience and that they have a lot to contribute to their child's education (Allen 2007; Freeman and Freeman 2001). The mother of a student who spoke Japanese went to Susan's class and taught the second graders how to write Japanese characters. The children were thrilled and eagerly showed me the characters they learned the next time I visited.

Another year, Susan invited a student's mother who had emigrated from Mexico and spoke no English to read a story in Spanish to the class (she also brought tamales for the children to try!). Subsequently, a number of children wrote about their own experiences with Mexico and other family members volunteered to come in to share stories, songs, and experiences with the students. These multilingual visits and experiences normalize multilingualism, extend children's understanding about other cultures, and help create strong school-family relationships. See Appendix B for a list of possible questions you can send home to invite these kinds of experiences in your classroom.

Figure 2.2

Including Multilingual Parents and Family Members

- Translate letters into the languages your students' families feel most comfortable communicating. Ask school personnel or community members for assistance. Also websites such as www.google.translate.com and www.babelfish.com, while not perfect, are helpful.

- Ask family members if they would like to teach a language lesson, talk about their home countries, share a hobby, or talk about their professions.

- Let parents know that you can get a translator, they can bring a friend or family member to help translate, or their child may help with translation.

- Arrange several after-school events where children share their work so parents can see your interest in their children and in their academic success.

- Send an interest inventory home for parents to complete (see Appendix B for some suggestions).

- Send home photos of children taken during school so you convey positive things the children are doing at school, like independent reading, helping others, conducting science experiments, writing, etc.

- Invite families to visit during writing time and to confer with students in their first languages.

- Ask parents what time of day/evening is most convenient for them to come to school, and also offer to meet them outside of school. One teacher I know often met parents at a local store where they frequently shopped; the families felt more comfortable meeting there than at the school.

- Invite parents to participate in a photography project (see page 30 for suggestions).

- Write a classroom newsletter with students, inviting them to write in languages other than English.

- Consider home visits. Many educators find that conducting home visits is often the first step to breaking down barriers between school and community. (See Allen 2007; López-Robertson et al. 2010 for suggestions and details.)

Build a Multilingual, Multicultural Classroom Library

Another way to ensure that students experience a range of cultures and languages in your classroom is your most important writing tool: your classroom library. In books, students find not only themselves—in stories, opinions, ideas, and information that matter to them—but also writing mentors. Multilingual children need to see their own identities being treated as valuable in the classroom's collection of reading material. They need access to texts in their primary languages as well as to texts that accurately reflect their cultures. Building an identity as a literate person means finding texts that resonate with your life. What this *doesn't* mean is that a child from Guatemala reads only texts about Guatemala. We need to expand our notion of "a variety of texts" to include not just genres and reading levels but also a variety of cultures and languages. This expanded notion of text variety reflects our values as a community: every child in that classroom understands the value of reading texts from and about numerous countries and cultures.

But we must make wise choices. These texts should offer models of who our students want to be. The Nigerian writer Chimamanda Adichie warns of the danger of a "single story" (www.ted.com/talks/chimamanda_adichie_the_danger_of_a_single_story.html). She argues that when books and stories "show people as one thing over and over again, then that is what they become" and that reading stories with negative portrayals of a people or culture "is to flatten [our] experience." We need to evaluate our classroom library as a whole and then each text individually to make sure we are not perpetuating stereotypes. (It helps to have some models of the kinds of texts we should offer children; see Appendix C for a list of such books.)

Creating a Multilingual, Multicultural Classroom Library

- **Evaluate your classroom library.** Which groups and cultures are represented? Who's missing? How are certain groups and cultures represented? What potential stereotypes are here? Do the portrayals reflect a wide variety of cultures, languages, and characters in a positive light?

TRY THIS

■ **Incorporate books in children's first languages.** Even if you do not speak students' home language(s), you can send home books for family members, caregivers, and other community members to read with children and ask for their feedback on the value of the book. This feedback can help you be mindful of translations or books that code-switch (insert words in other languages, such as Spanish) that may not use the same vocabulary that your students would use.

SOME ONLINE RESOURCES FOR MULTILINGUAL AND MULTICULTURAL TITLES

- www.wowlit.org reviews a wide array of multicultural and international children's literature
- www.leeandlow.com (Lee & Low publishers) publishes many multicultural children's literature books
- en.childrenslibrary.org provides books scanned and translated into multiple languages
- www.cincopuntos.com is an independent book publisher with many bilingual titles for children

Writing Is Connected to Writer's Lives

Asking our multilingual students to write about their lives is essential to inviting them into a classroom writing community in which we learn with and from one another. Beginning with the personal creates a meaningful foundation for multilingual students as they move into other kinds of writing, such as persuasive and informational writing. Emphasizing personal connections and topic choices does not mean that multilingual students solely write personal narratives; rather, they write about topics that matter to them. In the next few pages, you'll find many relevant ideas because this needs to be a thread of your students' writing throughout the year. It shouldn't just happen at the beginning of the year. Students can disengage for various reasons throughout the year, and activities like these help to remind them that who they are is essential to their writing identity.

Interest Inventories

Interest inventories are one tool for gathering potential topics for writing and help-ing students get to know one another as a community.

Creating and Using Interest Inventories

- There are plenty of premade interest inventories on the Internet and in profes-sional literature (see Appendix D for some sample questions). I use them as examples and then create my own questions about hobbies; travel; chores; lan-guages spoken, read, and written; TV shows; favorite games and sports; siblings. I might ask younger children to draw a picture of what they like to do at home. I might ask older students to think about a time they loved learning something, who taught them, and how they now use what they learned.

- Once the inventories are complete, identify common interests to create writing partnerships or connect what students are passionate about to district and state standards as you create curriculum.

- Inventories sent home for families to complete should be in the language in which the family feels most comfortable communicating. Children in the upper grades can fill them out themselves or interview one another (some may need a translator).

"Where I'm From" Poems

Many teachers use George Ella Lyon's poem "Where I'm From" to elicit powerful writing from students (Christensen 2002). Outside the writing workshop, the poem can generate conversations about experiences, relationships, and personal histories. Within the writing workshop, verbal and written responses to the poem are a great resource for more personal writing, like memoir. The list structure of the poem is accessible at all literacy levels and allows writers to draw from any linguistic reper-toire—regional dialects, Spanish, Chinese, you name it.

Kyleen Jackson said she learned more about her fifth graders in the three days she spent introducing the poem and helping them write their own innovations on it than she had in weeks of getting-to-know-you activities. Her students wrote about family members still in Mexico, grandparents in Brazil, funerals they attended, time spent in the family's nail salon each day after school, and foods they loved. They incorporated different languages and dialects—Spanish, African American language, and Portuguese. The poems became a touchstone throughout the year. Examples from previous years let students see how others responded to this invitation to write.

Using "Where I'm From"

- Read the poem aloud. Ask students what they notice about how it's structured and about the kinds of things George Ella Lyon includes in her list.

- Keep track of the categories students identify on a chart so that this list can become a scaffold for students' writing later on. Be sure to let them know that their poems shouldn't be limited by the kinds of things listed in George Ella Lyon's poem.

- Make sure students notice the different kinds of language in the poem: "know-it-alls," "Perk up! and Pipe down!" "He restoreth my soul," and use that as an invitation for them to incorporate nicknames, family sayings, different languages, and dialects.

- Ask students to share their examples orally. This serves as "writing in the air," helping children imagine what they may include in their own work.

George Ella Lyon's website—www.georgeellalyon.com—contains examples of similar poems from all over the world, as well as more ideas for teaching the poem.

Linda Christensen's essay in *Rethinking Schools* (2001) is another great resource for teaching strategies using this poem.

Heart Maps

Heart maps (Heard 1999) are illustrations that capture the geography of our hearts—the things we hold most dear. I especially love using heart maps at the beginning of the year because there is no performance pressure and there are so many ways to create them. Heart maps can contain drawings, single words, words or phrases in the student's primary language—anything that represents something that matters to the student. Like "Where I'm From" poems, heart maps are not something to worry over. They are not published, in the traditional sense, although putting them on a bulletin board at the beginning of the year is a great way to learn about one another and creates a powerful invitation for conversation among the school community. Examples of heart maps are shown in Figures 2.3A and 2.3B.

Creating Heart Maps

- **Talk about how writers regularly look inside their hearts for significant writing topics,** things that are important to them. I tell students that their heart map will be a source of writing inspiration throughout the year. I always create my own heart map, modeling the many kinds of representations students can

Figure 2.3A

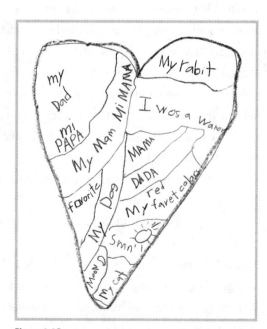

Figure 2.3B

use: drawings, single words, words or phrases in the student's first language. I want multilingual students to know that drawings are OK, as well as words in other languages. I often use Spanish when I make my heart map in order to provide an explicit demonstration.

- **Ask families to collaborate on heart maps to help create a stronger school-family connection.**

- **Students can create heart maps that identify things outside their heart—things they do not hold dear.** In upper elementary classrooms, this invitation has led to dynamic discussions about war, joblessness, and racism and extends the invitation to read, write, and talk about the fact that writers also address significant social issues.

Photographs from Home

Photographs reinforce the idea that children's lives are worth exploring and writing about. They ground students in the specifics of a particular moment in time (a great tool for writing). A photograph can be a wonderful tool for sparking a conversation with students who speak little or no English. We can point to a photo and ask students how to say things in the language they speak, then spell the words phonetically or in children's first language, and then translate it into English. Students can tell stories about these photos to other children who speak the same language they do. We can also scaffold student talk by naming what we notice, "Look at your baby sister. It looks like you are hugging her . . ." If students do not have photographs, remind them that memories and images in our minds can be drawn and talked about as though they were photos.

During a memoir unit, Ms. Rojas and I invited her third-grade multilingual students to bring photos to school so we could talk about their childhood memories. Graciela brought an entire baby book, which her classmates loved looking through and giggling at pictures of the baby brother they had heard so much about. Felipe did not have photos, so he sketched a memory in his writer's notebook—a drawing of the *tienda* (store) in Mexico where his grandparents worked and lived. The students knew how much Felipe missed his family in Mexico, and they asked him to tell about what he did there when he last visited. Conversations like these can be an essential first step, a kind of "writing in the air"—a scaffold for writing in print later.

TRY THIS

Incorporating Photographs as a Scaffold for "Writing in the Air"

Ask students to bring a photograph, or a sketch of a memory, to your next morning meeting. Let them know that they need to be prepared to explain the image to the class. They should also be prepared to ask questions about other students' photographs. Include concrete and abstract questions. Give students some example questions the day before and record them on a classroom chart:

- "Who is in this picture?"

- "What is happening in this picture?"

- "Where was this picture taken?"

- "When you look at that photograph [or drawing], how does it make you feel?"

- "Why is this photograph special to you?"

- "What are some important details you want us to notice?"

For writing partners:

- "What do you notice is different in your pictures?"

- "What is the same in your pictures?"

These questions will help your students prepare to talk about their photos and prepare for future writing.

Taking Pictures to Document Our Lives

Photographs (taken with a digital or disposable camera) link children's home life to the classroom in a less abstract way than heart maps do. Students become photographers—they choose what to photograph and which photographs to keep. Seeing an accumulation of photographs that tell a story helps students recognize that their identity is not one-dimensional but layered. Given a little guidance on what and how to photograph, students will capture authentic reflections of their lives.

For a family photography project that was part of a fall poetry unit, second-grade teacher Susan emphasized the importance of taking candid shots of family members going about their daily lives. The photographs that came back showed children playing video games, holding baby siblings, chasing soccer balls, reading with a grandmother in Arabic, cooking rice and beans, and painting houses with their fathers—children in a "complex and engaging web of social relationships" (Allen et al. 2002, 322). Recognizing the rich resource her students had created, Susan encouraged them to return to these photographs when they wrote in other genres as well.

Julian, who spoke Spanish and English, had photographed the chickens he raised in his backyard, along with other photos of his family. His knowledge of chickens became the topic of Julian's poetry, memoir, and nonfiction writing. (See Figure 2.4 for Julian's poem about his family, inspired by his chicken photos.) His passion for raising chickens was inextricably linked to his identity and his literacy development as a writer. By using a camera throughout the year, students understand that identity grows and changes and that the pictures they take and the pieces they write can reflect that growth and change.

MY FAMILY

My mom is nice to me
She makes me Spanish food
I see her cooking on the stove
She cooks and I smile
My sisters make me happy
When they sit and watch me
With their dark cat eyes

My dad works hard
It makes me happy when
He comes home with his t-shirt
Stretching out like a tall oak tree
Smelling like a new building he just built
My chicks play and throw
Their food with their long legs
Like the vines and
Scream like girls like they're mummies
trying to attack
My family is nice to me

Figure 2.4 Julian's poem

Getting Cameras for This Project

Getting supplies like cameras is often a challenge, but I'm always surprised by the solutions teachers find when they lack material resources. For this project, my university students each bought a disposable camera, and children had the opportunity to use the entire supply in their classroom at some time during the year. The immediacy of a digital camera makes it possible for all students in a class to share it. Families who live near one another may be willing to share cameras. Some teachers use Donors Choose (www.donorschoose.org) to request materials. (For additional sources of external funding, see Appendix E.) However we are able to bring a photography project to life, it is an invaluable teaching tool that supports writing, information gathering/research, and storytelling throughout the year.

Self-Portraits

Self-portraits are another powerful writing scaffold for multilingual students; they can use color, line, and shape to communicate emotion and self-perception. The third-grade teachers in a school at which I consulted asked the art teacher to take black-and-white photos of all the third graders early in the year (the students were invited to choose their own props, such as scarves or masks). In art class, each student colored over his or her photograph, explaining what each color meant and how it represented his or her identity. The teachers then had the students use these self-portraits as inspiration during a poetry unit. The poem below was inspired by the photograph in Figure 2.5.

Figure 2.5

BIG BROTHER
by Juan

I have to read to my sister and brother
So they can sleep at night.
When they wake up,
I give them breakfast

So they can eat something
I take my sister to school
I go to school
We go to the bus.
When I go to the bus
I miss my brother so much
But when I come back from school
He runs and hugs me.
I
LIKE TO
BE
A BIG
BROTHER

Self-portraits can also be used during memoir studies. See Katherine Bomer's wonderful book *Writing a Life* (2005) for more ideas.

Community: An Essential Mindset for Learning

When our multilingual students understand that they are part of a community of writers who respect and reflect their multilingual identities, we've established an essential mindset for learning. In a time of curriculum mandates, one thing we do have control over is the kind of classroom community we create. For children to feel like a part of this community, to feel ready to take risks and learn, our classrooms need to be places in which children are allowed to speak in their first language. Professional literature is filled with heartbreaking stories of multilingual children who were denied this right (Reyes 2011). I have seen children who loved speaking Spanish in kindergarten then deny their Spanish fluency by the time they were in third grade. When we ask multilingual children to leave significant aspects of their identity at the school door, we risk losing them altogether. That is too high a price to pay.

If we truly value our children, we need to demonstrate that we value what they know: we must draw on children's existing linguistic and cultural resources as we prepare our curriculum. There is an inextricable link between learning and identity, and our classroom and the behavior in it needs to invite multilingual children to share, read, write, and fully participate. In a classroom where being multilingual is common and children feel valued and recognized for who they are—competent, capable human beings—we have a much better chance of creating a learning environment in which multilingual children succeed.

What Can This Look Like?

The following are some observations I made of two multilingual students, using the tools explained in this chapter. As I emphasize cultivating multilingual writers in this book, I want you to see how our writing is a resource for our instruction. By writing down what we observe and recording information using various tools, we are then able to reflect on our observations and make informed curricular decisions that consider students as whole, complex people.

In Figures 2.6A and 2.6B, I share the notes I gathered in a notebook where I recorded information from a range of tools and resources. Record keeping is individual and idiosyncratic. I like to keep a notebook with a tab for each student, but I know other teachers who use one sheet per week with every child's name on it. That way they can record observations about the class for the week and can ensure that they have information about every child. I urge you to design a record-keeping and observation system that works well for you. I share mine only to give you a peek into my observation practices and how these notes inform my teaching decisions. The short paragraph reflects what I have learned thus far about these two third-grade students through interest inventories, stories told during morning meeting, impromptu conversations, and classroom observations.

Pulling all these ideas together can seem overwhelming, but I want you to notice how these tools and strategies inform observation and planning over a period of time. Effective teaching is cumulative, and taking these kinds of records and notes helps to make an explicit and recurrent link between identity and instruction. As you read through the rest of these chapters, I hope you'll see how this practice accelerates multilingual writers' growth.

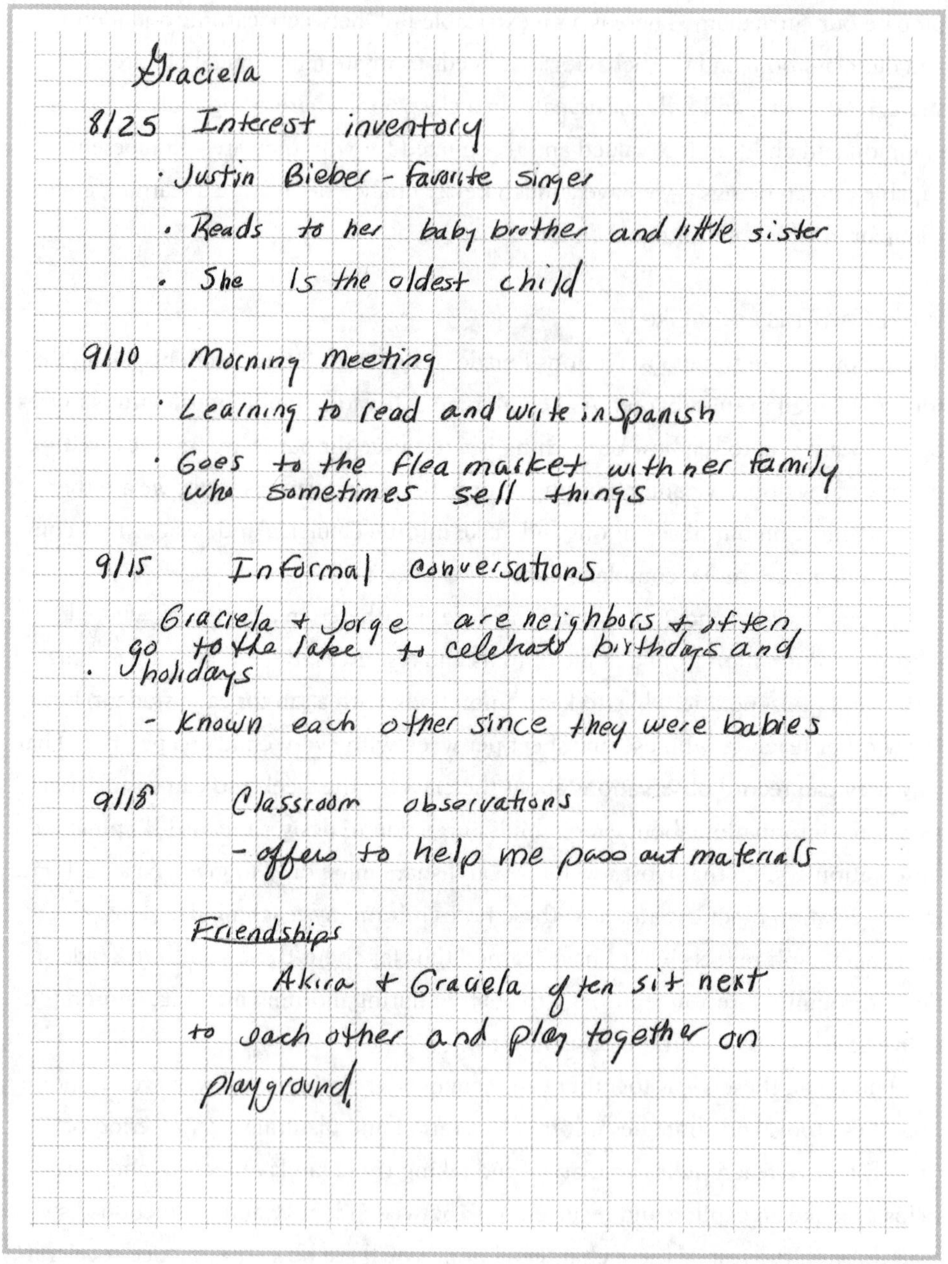

Graciela

8/25   Interest inventory
    · Justin Bieber - favorite singer
    · Reads to her baby brother and little sister
    · She is the oldest child

9/10   Morning meeting
    · Learning to read and write in Spanish
    · Goes to the flea market with her family
      who sometimes sell things

9/15   Informal conversations
    Graciela + Jorge are neighbors + often
  go to the lake to celebrate birthdays and
· holidays
    - known each other since they were babies

9/18   Classroom observations
    - offers to help me pass out materials

    Friendships
      Akira + Graciela often sit next
  to each other and play together on
  playground.

Figure 2.6A

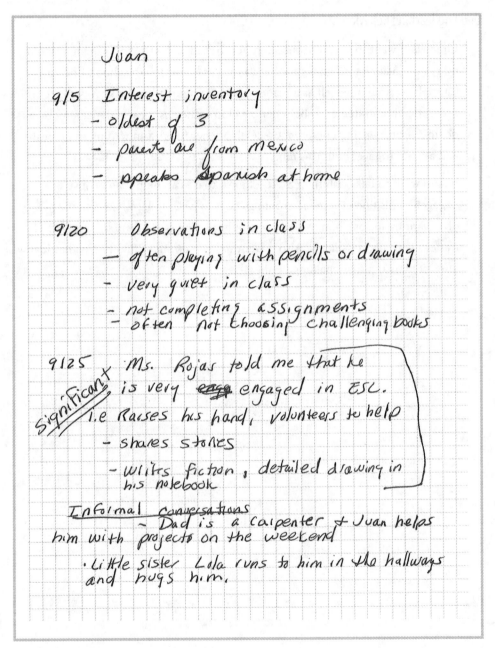

Juan

9/5   Interest inventory
        - oldest of 3
        - parents are from Mexico
        - speaks Spanish at home

9/20   Observations in class
            - often playing with pencils or drawing
            - very quiet in class
            - not completing assignments
            - often not choosing challenging books

9/25   Significant   Ms. Rojas told me that he
                is very ~~easy~~ engaged in ESL.
                i.e Raises his hand, volunteers to help
            - shares stories
            - writes fiction, detailed drawing in
              his notebook

        Informal conversations
                - Dad is a carpenter & Juan helps
        him with projects on the weekend
            · Little sister Lola runs to him in the hallways
            and hugs him.

Figure 2.6B

Ongoing Teaching Behaviors

Graciela: I want to keep encouraging her to read and write in Spanish. Bring in more bilingual picture books for her to read at home and in school. Encourage Graciela to stretch herself as a reader. Listen to her read and take miscue notes in order to guide strategies to help her develop strategies for when meaning breaks down. During writing conferences, celebrate her interest in writing in Spanish and ask her to talk about this more.

Juan: I want to talk with the ESL teacher so that I can help Juan be just as engaged in his homeroom classroom as he is in ESL. Talk to Juan about my observations and ask him to share one of his fiction stories and his detailed illustrations with his classmates. Also, I want to keep trying to find books that Juan is interested in and that challenge him.

3

Minilessons

**A Story of
Instruction
That Includes
All Writers**

It can feel like a leap when we begin writing workshop with multilingual children. We worry whether we are designing curriculum that meets our students' individual and collective needs. Ms. Rodríguez, an English as a Second Language teacher, had similar concerns when she decided to implement writing workshop. Ms. Rodríguez had fifteen multilingual kindergarten students with an array of languages such as Arabic, Chinese, Japanese, Spanish, and Finnish. As many of her students were newcomers to English, she worried that asking them to write would intimidate and alienate them.

But Ms. Rodríguez did not let that fear stop her from taking a risk that she believed would benefit her multilingual students. She read professional books, consulted more experienced writing workshop teachers, and jumped in. Four days a week, Ms. Rodríguez called her students to the rug in front of her classroom. Below is one of Ms. Rodríguez's first minilessons. Notice how even first attempts at this kind of instruction carry significant, positive implications for multilingual writers' growth. Later in the chapter, I share another minilesson to show the range of lessons we teach to multilingual students over time.

CONNECTION

I am so proud of you! You did a really good job yesterday. Yesterday we thought of many things we can write. We can write about our family, our friends, playing. We can write about our houses, our vacations, and our friends. Remember, first we drew our picture (*Ms. Rodríguez points to the picture she drew*). When we finished drawing, we wrote about our picture (*makes a gesture as though she is writing*).

TEACHING POINT

Yesterday, I heard some of you say, "I'm done!" I'm going to tell you a secret: You know what writers do? Sometimes, when they think they are done, they are just beginning. Remember yesterday I told you I was sick last week? Remember I couldn't write about Stefan's mom because I don't know her well? So I wrote about something I do know—I wrote about being sick. (*Ms. Rodríguez points to the writing sample she did the day before*). I wrote: *Last week I was sick. I did not come to school.*

I could add more to my writing. I could tell you what I did when I was sick and lying in my bed. I watched *El Chavo del Ocho*. I know some of you also watch that television show. (*Ms. Rodríguez then begins to write and points to each word as she writes it and reads it aloud*). I'm going to write this (*El Chavo del Ocho*) in Spanish because the show is in Spanish. Read it with me. (*The students read it in unison*.) (See Figure 3.1.)

STUDENT ENGAGEMENT

Think about something more you want to tell about your picture, just like I did. Talk to each other and tell each other what you could add to your story from yesterday. (*Ms. Rodríguez and Ms. Garner, her assistant, move around to each student pair and listen to them.*)

Ms. Rodríguez: OK, what are some things you thought about that you could add?
Evelyn: We went to the hospital and waited for my Mommy.
Ms. Rodríguez: Oh, you are going to add that you had to wait for your Mommy when she was sick.

Figure 3.1

OFF YOU GO

When you go to write today, remember, look at your pictures and think to yourself, "What else can I add?" Then write some more words so your reader knows more about your story.

The teaching point of this minilesson—writers adding details to their writing—may seem small, but it is such big and important work for these children who are just embarking on their journeys as writers. When I unpack this lesson by examining Ms. Rodríguez's talk and her action, I notice the following teaching moves she makes to support her multilingual students:

- She begins with a narrative story about yesterday's work.

- She uses a visual cue to remind students of the writing she demonstrated yesterday.

- She provides a verbal demonstration for her students, modeling English syntax.

- Her tone is inclusive, and she talks to her students like fellow writers.

- She writes about a Spanish-language television show that most of her children know and watch.

- She points to each word and has the children read with her, demonstrating concepts of print that are significant for children learning to read in English.

- She asks students to turn and talk to their partners, which provides her multilingual students the opportunity to try out their ideas with a partner before speaking to the whole group.

- She models her writing and writes in Spanish, which validates the majority of her students' language(s).

- She checks for understanding.

- She verbalizes the internal question that children can ask themselves when they complete their writing.

The Big Work of Minilessons

Our minilessons, though brief, do big work. They give us the opportunity to teach directly, clearly, succinctly, and meaningfully. Minilessons also engage multilingual learners by inviting them into the world of words and showing students that writing is indeed hard work, but they are becoming insiders to the process. This stands in contrast to other kinds of whole-group instruction where multilingual students are often on the periphery of classroom instruction or where the instruction is based on that banking model of education I wrote about in Chapter 2: filling in blanks, answering questions they already know the answer to, and never trying to apply new content to their own work.

In contrast, all the content of a minilesson—the strategies, processes, and craft—is explicitly linked to communicating significance. In a minilesson, students learn the ritual of writing. This structure creates a sense of predictability and safety and ensures that students feel equipped for the independent writing that follows the minilesson. This allows students to take risks and stretch their writing selves. The most effective minilessons follow a structure: connection, teaching point, student engagement, and send off (Anderson 2000; Calkins 1994).

For the teacher of multilingual students, the planned, explicit instruction of a minilesson provides an opportunity to refine our language to be more inclusive and supportive. In this chapter, I'll take you through each part of a minilesson and offer some strategies that are particularly helpful for multilingual students and that help us make the most of this brief teaching time. Then you'll see a transcript of a minilesson as it applies some of the strategies in a multilingual classroom. To conclude, you'll see a broad view: how a series of minilessons can tell a curricular story that you can be mindful of as you try to meet the diversity of language learners in your own classroom.

Acknowledging Multilingual Writing and Writers in the Connection

All minilessons begin with a *connection* (Calkins 1994; Anderson 2000). The connection recognizes that students already have life experiences that will help them grow their understanding of writing. This makes it an ideal place to acknowledge our multilingual students' identities and their resources. The connection situates our students' learning within a narrative: what have we been doing in writing, what do we plan to teach them today, and how are yesterday and today linked together?

The connection should incorporate strategies that acknowledge and support your multilingual students. Although you might not feel like you can accomplish this in every minilesson, you can with some practice. Start by trying one strategy in a minilesson this week. Because the connection is so brief, I'm presenting the strategies in a chart so you can see model sentences of the strategy in action (see Table 3.1).

Launch Multilingual Writers into Something They Can Do Right Away

This part of the lesson is crucial to students' success, but it is also important not to do too much. We want our teaching to be concise for multilingual students. Research shows that the most effective minilesson makes only one teaching point (Calkins 1994). This focus helps us to quickly demonstrate a writing strategy before asking students to get involved. The other key piece to a successful teaching point

Connections That Work for Multilingual Students

STRATEGY	HOW IT MAY SOUND...
Choose shared multicultural, multilingual literature as mentor texts.	Remember when we read *Friends from the Other Side / Amigos del otro Lado*, and we talked about how Gloria Anzaldúa, the author, made us think about how each of her characters saw the world from their perspective?
Connect students' languages to key instructional words.	We are studying memoir. *Memoir* is a story that we tell about our lives, based on our memories. In Spanish, *recuerdos* or *memorias*, means "memories," right?
Embed the definition of key words into instruction.	Writers, today we are going to talk about *revision* and how we *change* our writing.
Make the connection relevant to current events in your community.	We are writing stories about our lives. I heard some of you talking about the Latin Festival this weekend, and I heard Xavier talking about the long line at the taco truck and the band La Mariposa. Those of you who went to the festival this weekend could write about that. Here are some other things you have shared lately . . .
Explain that it is necessary for writers to write in the language that feels most fluent, even if they later translate the text. This helps students to see their language(s) as a resource.	I noticed Marie is writing her story in Spanish first. Many writers do this because it is easier to think of what you want to say or how you want to say it. Sometimes writers do this because the person they are writing for reads Spanish (Chinese, Japanese).
Develop students' meta-awareness of their own language processes.	We've been talking about how our brains work and how sometimes you may think in Chinese and other times you think in English. Today we will talk about how we may also do that in our writing—sometimes you may think in Chinese, so it is easier to write in Chinese. Sometimes you may think in English, and it may feel easier to write in English. Or sometimes you may think in both languages, going back and forth. As you are writing today, pay attention to when you think in English and when you think in other language(s).
Bring your life into the classroom.	Remember how I always tell you that I like the city more than the country? Remember how I like it when you tell me stories about your pets, although I am a little scared of some animals? Well this summer, I went to the country to visit friends who have a farm and a lot of animals.

Table 3.1

is demonstration, a condition Brian Cambourne (1995) identified as essential to learning: children must observe someone engaged in what the child is learning. For this reason, this portion of the minilesson is often direct and explicit. It also immerses students in the real work of writing by first providing strong demonstrations for them. Ask yourself these questions to ensure your teaching points support your multilingual writers.

Questions to Ask Yourself . . .
When Planning Teaching Points

- Is my teaching point connected to the ongoing work we have been doing?

- Is there any new vocabulary that my multilingual students need to know?

- Are there any terms that I need to learn in students' languages in order to teach this content?

- Am I avoiding idiomatic expressions that multilingual students may not understand?

- Am I speaking at an appropriate pace, given my students' levels of English proficiency?

- Do I have a mentor text (mine, a student's, or published) that will illustrate my teaching point? Does this mentor text reflect my students' cultural and linguistic resources?

- Would gestures or a fishbowl help to make this teaching point more accessible to multilingual students?

- Do I rephrase or repeat my teaching point so that students have multiple opportunities to make meaning?

- What visuals (charts, illustrations, photographs, steps) are helpful for sharing this information?

Incorporating Conventional Spelling

Sarah, a first-grade teacher, taught an early minilesson inspired by Katie Wood Ray (2004). It was designed to help her students take risks in their writing by spelling words the best they could by stretching sounds. This chart (see Figure 3.2) hung in the room for most of the year as Sarah returned again and again to the idea that writers spell words the best they can and later find the conventional spelling.

This is an important lesson for multilingual students because it explicitly teaches children that approximation is the expectation for learning. Over the years, Sarah has seen that some multilingual students' concerns with perfection prevent them from producing very much text or taking risks with spelling when students know the word they want to use but are unsure of its spelling.

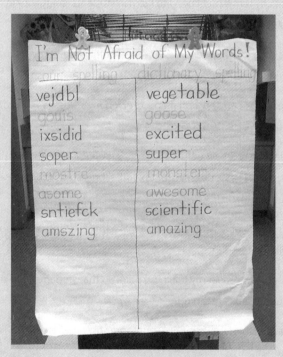

Figure 3.2

Demonstrate Ideas and Reinforce New Language with Images

When we *show* students, rather than just telling them, they are able to observe our thinking in action and to connect it to a visual. Creating charts during minilessons serves as an effective visual support for multilingual students. Better yet, referring to those charts, linking images from previous days, and then adding a small amount of text can help students have a better chance of understanding the minilesson because multilingual students can rely on the visual as they build their language. Ms. Kelly, a first-grade teacher, created a chart when she introduced writing workshop to her first graders. She took pictures of the children during each part of the workshop and then hung the chart in the room for the remainder of the year.

Gestures

When working with multilingual students who are emergent English speakers and writers, gestures serve as a visual emphasis for conveying meaning. For instance, when you introduce writing workshop to your students, you may create a chart with *think*, *picture or draw*, and *write* as steps in the process. It may be helpful to accompany those three ideas with gestures: pointing to your head to demonstrate thinking, moving your hand over paper to illustrate drawing, and using a pencil or marker to show writing.

Dramatic Interpretations

In addition to using gestures in instruction, dramatic interpretations by students can be particularly engaging for all students and give multilingual students context clues that they may have missed otherwise. For example, when I read *In My Family / En mi familia* by Carmen Lomas Garza in a third-grade classroom, several children familiar with piñatas helped dramatize how people are blindfolded and then use a stick to hit a piñata during birthday celebrations. We even had a piñata for students to use during their dramatic reenactment, which helped students who were unfamiliar with this cultural practice.

Mentor Texts

When we create and/or share models of the kinds of texts we are asking our students to write, we are providing one model among many that multilingual children may

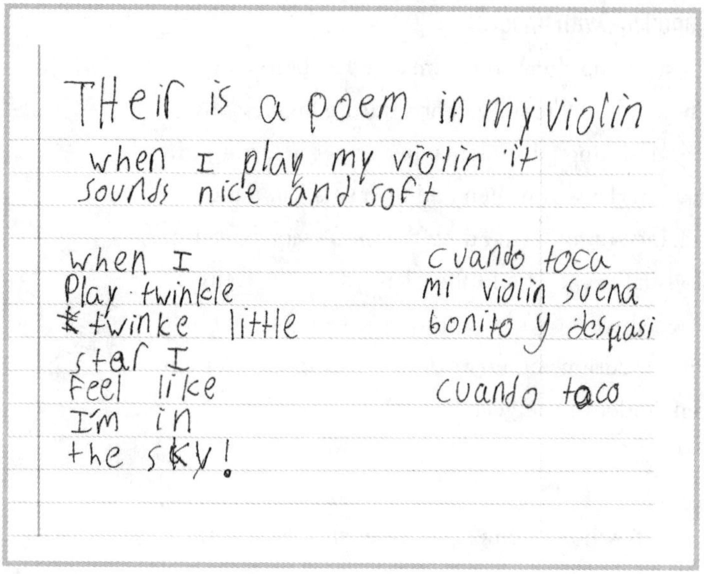

THeir is a poem in my violin
when I play my violin it
sounds nice and soft

when I
Play twinkle
twinke little
star I
Feel like
I'm in
the sky!

Cuando toca
mi violin suena
bonito y despasi

Cuando taco

Figure 3.3

turn to in order to understand what we are teaching them. This is one of the most effective practices for building independent writers in our classrooms. Ms. Rodríguez, a kindergarten teacher, always creates the same kinds of texts that her children are writing. She then uses these model texts during minilessons to point out text features and structures, to remind children about key teaching points she has previously made, and to

give them an example of the kind of writing work that they are doing—just as she did in the minilesson at the beginning of this chapter (see Figure 3.1).

Student Models

Using student models is also helpful; they are usually closer to the kinds of writing that students will produce. When second-grade teacher Susan Ross introduced students to poetry, she shared poems from her previous students (see Figure 3.3). The children were delighted to hear the poems since they knew many of the students. Susan read poems that included Spanish so her students knew this was a possibility for their writing as well.

Bilingual Texts

Multilingual students need to see us take risks with language learning, just as we expect them to take risks each day as they learn to read, write, and speak English. It is so important to have bilingual books incorporated into your minilessons and to take time to share them with your students. During a memoir unit, I planned to share a page from Carmen Lomas Garza's bilingual picture book *In My Family / En mi familia* with Ms. Rojas' third graders in order to show them that the author remembered many ordinary things from her childhood to create this book filled with childhood memories and that we could do the same thing from our own lives—draw from the everyday to craft memoirs. When I opened the book and turned to the page about how Lomas Garza and her family celebrated birthdays, Graciela said, "Hey, there are words in Spanish there!" Juan said, "Will you read it to us?" "Of course," I said, "As long as you help me with some of the pronunciation, because I don't know how to say some of the words."

My attempts at reading Spanish and enlisting the children's help gave them better access to the point I was trying to make about writing from one's everyday life. It took just a couple of minutes to read the text, but that extra two minutes was time well spent because some of the children said, "Oh, now the English part makes sense." This interaction reminded me how often our multilingual students may not entirely understand what we are teaching them, despite their conversational proficiency (Freeman and Freeman 2007; Gibbons 2002). For weeks afterward, children came to tell me how they were learning to read and write in Spanish, Chinese, or Japanese, and how they were now asking their parents to teach them to write in their home languages.

Pattern Books

When Ms. Rodríguez's kindergarten students were creating pattern books, she and the children read a number of pattern books and then created a list of the patterns they found in the books (see Figure 3.4).

Some children then chose to use these patterns, while others created their own as Joe did, a student whose first language is Chinese. He chose to extend one of the patterns to "I can read" (see Figure 3.5).

This particular student engagement was powerful for several students who were newcomers to English because it taught a basic sentence pattern that was easily repeated, and

Pattern Phrases

I see
I can
My feet
Have you seen
It looked like

Figure 3.4

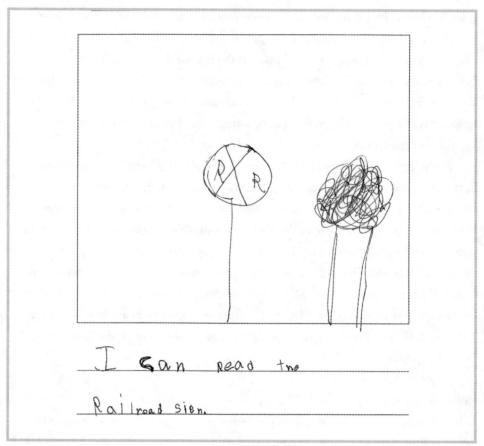

I can read the
Railroad sign.

Figure 3.5

then students could add a word or two to complete the sentence. With this scaffold, students are able to feel successful in a short amount of time.

Cultivate an Atmosphere of Risk-Taking and Engagement

Because we don't usually require students to implement the strategy or skill we taught in the minilesson during their independent writing time, it is necessary to take some time (even if brief) for students to *have a go* (Anderson 2000), or try out what we just taught. Going back to Cambourne's (1995) conditions of learning, *engagement*—actually doing the thing you are learning about—is essential for learning.

Engagement does just that by allowing students to try the thinking actions that inform writing. This portion of the minilesson often entails talking in groups of two or three or sharing with the whole group or referring to writing that students have already done. Very rarely do students produce any kind of new writing during this part of the minilesson, simply because it takes too much time away from students' independent work time.

In planning this portion of the minilesson, we need to consider the risks students are taking to "try on" what we are teaching. We also need to make sure students know that we do not expect perfection, but rather we expect *approximation* and trial and error. This is a special consideration when teaching multilingual students, who, I observe, are often worried about "getting it right." Learning anything is just not that smooth or easy. When we invite children to try something we've taught, it is a time for them to imagine how this skill, strategy, or new idea fits into what they already know about writing. There are structures we can incorporate during this part of the minilesson to support and encourage multilingual students and that make trying, failing, and approximation intrinsic to how learning happens in our writing communities and exactly what we expect.

Turn and Talk: All Minds Engaged

For a child who does not yet feel confident speaking English, sharing with a partner or the whole group can feel daunting, but there is much we can do to alleviate this kind of anxiety. Turning and talking to one or two people is a powerful talk structure in multilingual classrooms because every child gets to speak without everyone looking at them. For some multilingual students, talking with one other person is less intimidating than talking in front of the whole group. Some teachers have students simply turn and talk to the person next to them, while other teachers have planned writing partnerships. Inviting students to talk with their partners (either their neighbor or their assigned partner) in their home language(s) in order to demonstrate their understanding is one way for multilingual students to share with one another and to lower student anxiety. We can also teach students how to support one another during turn and talk by teaching students to repeat what their partner says, elaborating on their partner's responses, asking questions, and providing words that their partner needs.

Inquiry: Let's Be Uncertain and Curious Together

Some minilessons take longer because we want students to do some inquiry work during the student engagement portion of the minilesson. This usually means we want students to study a text for particular text features or to study craft in small groups. During a nonfiction study, we may ask students to look through nonfiction texts and use self-stick notes to mark pages where they notice how the text looks different from other books. When second graders in Susan's classroom did this they put self-stick notes on headers, labels, diagrams, the table of contents, glossaries, and bold print, all before they ever began thinking about writing nonfiction. These kinds of guided inquiries allow students to work with others, and they help us monitor multilingual students' understanding of the teaching point and provide support where necessary.

Questions to Ask Yourself . . .
as You Plan Your Student Engagement for Multilingual Learners

- Will practicing first in the students' home language(s) help them before they try in English?

- Would a chart provide a reference for multilingual students to refer to during this time?

- Do students have classroom friends or partners they can talk to in their home language(s)?

- Is there a nonverbal way for students to demonstrate their understanding (thumbs up, raising hands, holding up an example)?

Send-off: You're Ready to Try It Out

There is a link between student engagement and students going to write during independent writing time. This send-off is the metaphorical "note on the refrigerator," where we reiterate our teaching point and remind students that they too can do this work and try it in their own writing when they go back to their seats. The send-off is intentional and serves as a link between the minilesson and students' independent writing time. I often use the send-off as a final place to check students' understanding.

Strategies for Send-off with Multilingual Students

- Have students reread their writing. As they do this, ask them to consider some focused questions, such as, "Is there a place where you could describe what you were thinking?" You could remind them of a mentor text you referenced in the lesson as an example.

- Have students refer to the charts you created as a class. If you modeled a certain chart in your lesson, use it in the send-off. For example, ask children to find a place where they wrote about a feeling, like "I am happy." Make a T-chart and write, tell, and show details they could add for their reader.

- Have students use snippets of first language or illustrations to enhance their story.

- Display phrases that students may use in their writing, and ask them to incorporate those phrases as they move into independent writing.

- Ask students to tell their writing partner what they are going to do today during independent writing time.

If We Think Students Can't Do Something, Then We Teach It

A common complaint about elementary students in general, and multilingual children in particular, is that their writing often lacks sufficient description and detail. That lack of detail is often blamed on multilingual children's English language proficiency. Sometimes we say things like, "I told them to add details, but they didn't do it." My favorite response to this statement is from Isoke Nia, a staff developer and writer, who says, "You're a teacher, not a teller," because it reminds me that if I notice something lacking in my students' writing and I blame their English language proficiency, then I am excusing myself from teaching. I'm also reinforcing a deficit model when in fact I need to figure out how to teach whatever my students need.

In the following minilesson, I address this very issue with Susan Ross' second graders who were learning how to take a small moment from a bigger story and develop it through details. This is not an easy idea to teach, and Susan thought this was just the study that would help her multilingual students with this second-grade curriculum standard. In the first few days, Susan read stories to the children, highlighting small moments. She had her children make timelines and then tell one story on the timeline. She wanted them to develop these narratives even more by describing how emotions feel, physically. Even in their storytelling, students would often say, "I was happy, I was sad, etc." Susan and I often plan units and minilessons together, and she asked me if I would mind teaching the lesson so she could watch her students and see what aspects of the lesson seemed most beneficial.

CONNECTION

Writers, yesterday you learned about making timelines from your lives and choosing something from your timeline to write more about. We've been learning about small moments. Small moments do not mean just a little bit of writing. They mean a lot of detail about just one thing that happened. (*Remind students what they did yesterday and what they have been studying and define small moment.*)

TEACHING POINT

Today I am going to show you how you can stretch out a small moment by showing and not telling. I am going to show you how you can describe for your readers how you felt by *showing* your emotions rather than just *telling* us your emotions. Remember, emotions are about feelings (sad, happy, scared, nervous). What do people look like when they are sad? Everyone show a sad face. On my timeline, I wrote about learning to drive a horse and carriage this summer. (*Draw a quick sketch of a horse and carriage so students know what it is.*) Look what I wrote (*put up the paper with my writing*). Listen for places where I just *tell* you how I feel:

> This summer, my friend Jack took Bob and me for a horse-and-carriage ride. The horse's name is Tom. He weighs 1,000 pounds, and he was more than six feet tall. I felt very small next to him. Jack and Pat sat in the front. Bob and I climbed in the back seat and we rode down a dirt road. It was dry and dusty and when Tom put his big hooves in the dirt, dust came up. The dirt was getting in my eyes and it was annoying me. I heard a car coming and I got scared, but the car was driving slowly and the driver just waved at us. Then Jack asked me if I wanted to drive the carriage. I was really nervous because I don't know anything about horses, but I decided to try anyway. I climbed in the front and sat next to Jack. He gave me the horse's reins and he said, "Pull left, Tasha" and when I did the horse went to the left. And then Jack said, "Pull right, Tasha" and I did and Tom went right. I was so happy! We went all the way through a big field with bales of hay rolled up that the horses would eat later in the summer. I loved learning how to drive a horse and carriage. I wonder what I will learn next?

(*Embed a definition of* emotions *in the teaching point. Check for understanding using physical demonstration. Have a written copy of the writing hanging up so students can see it as you read. Give students directions for what to listen for. Draw a quick sketch of a horse and carriage.*)

Remember, our emotions are how we feel. What are some of the emotions I have in my small moment? I am going to underline those words. Now, let me show you what writers do. Instead of just telling you I was scared, nervous, or happy, I can show you by adding details that describe my actions or the movements of my body. Watch. I am going to make a chart. I am writing my emotions on one side—my short sentence—and then, on the other side, I am going to say more about how I felt inside when I was nervous. Do you see the difference between the two? One sentence just says, "I was nervous," but the other side tells you how my heart fluttered and my hands sweated, and explains what I was worried about. You can really understand more about what was happening to me. (*Model example in front of students.*)

Telling	Showing
I was nervous.	When Jack asked me if I wanted to drive the carriage, I said yes, but my heart was fluttering because Tom is a very big horse. I wondered, "What if he won't listen to me? What if he runs away?" I climbed up front, next to Jack, and my hands were sweaty when I grabbed the leather reigns. Reigns are what you hold in your hands to direct the horse.

STUDENT ENGAGEMENT

Look at your timeline. What is something you are going to write about? Now think of an emotion you felt. How will you show the reader what you felt? Tell your neighbor. (*Teachers listen in.*) I heard Rosa say that she is going to write about being excited before her grandmother came and how she jumped up and down when she saw her grandmother walk through the airport.

(*Ask students to think of their own timeline and what they could say. Walk around and listen to students to elicit more information from them. Draw attention to something I overheard.*)

OFF YOU GO

Today when you go off to write, you can also make a chart. On one side you can write a short sentence about how you felt, and on the other side you can show your reader how you felt. When we come back for sharing time, if you tried this we'll have some of you show us your charts. (*Remind students of the strategy I showed them, invite them to try it, and reinforce that we will revisit the strategy again at sharing time.*) (See Figure 3.6 for an example of work from a student who tried this strategy.)

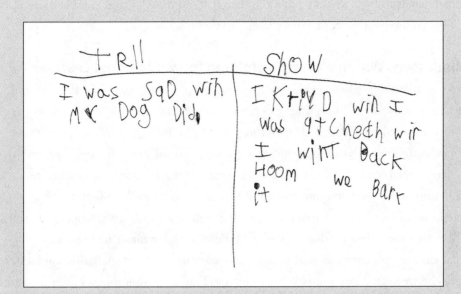

Figure 3.6

During writing time, Pablo tried the strategy taught during the minilesson. His telling sentence says, "I was sad when my dog died." On the Showing side of his chart, he wrote, "I cried when I was at church. When I went back home we buried it." Pablo, whose English language proficiency would be considered developing, and in some situations still emerging, was clearly able to add details to his writing by describing crying as well as what happened when he got home. Inside of his sentence, "I was sad when my dog died" is more story, waiting to be called forth through strong teaching.

When we came back together for sharing time, Ms. Ross asked Pablo, who was often shy, to share his writing with the class. Of course, the children responded to Pablo's sadness by sharing their own experiences with losing pets. But they also saw how Ms. Ross highlighted Pablo's work, which encouraged others to try their own hand at adding more details. This isn't to say that every child in the room suddenly added details to their writing, but more than half did that day and in subsequent days as they continued to practice this strategy in their own writing.

Minilessons Within a Unit: Scaffolding for Multilingual Learners

Isoke Nia says that when we plan units of study in a writing workshop there should be minilessons that fall into three categories: minilessons about writing process (collecting, choosing a seed idea, drafting, revising, editing, publishing), the "thing" we are currently studying (e.g., poetry, memoir, revision), and what our students currently need (adding more words to the page, paying attention to punctuation, gathering in their writer's notebooks, etc.). I often add a fourth column to these categories of minilessons when I am teaching multilingual students: language lessons. There are times when particular aspects of the English language are important to what students are currently writing, or I may want to highlight similarities and differences between students' primary languages and English. Other times, I want to share insights into other multilingual writers and their writing processes. (See Figure 3.8 at the end of this chapter.)

During a study of memoir, for example, I may point out that many memoirs are written in the past tense or that writing a memoir in language(s) other than English may be appropriate, depending on the author's intended audience. While teaching past tense to students who are completely new to English does not make sense, it does make sense for other students by illustrating this point in a rich learning context—by sharing many literary resources and then demonstrating it in our own writing. Showing students how to use their home language(s) as a placeholder so they do not lose their ideas for writing helps students use their language resources strategically. Language-focused minilessons are not the bulk of my units of study, and I share this idea with caution; I do not want you to think that you have to teach grammar in isolated ways or that multilingual students must master grammatical forms before they write entire stories. Instead, several short minilessons *connected to language* allow you to embed meaningful language instruction within the context of children's current writing projects, where necessary and appropriate.

The Power of Shared Language and Demonstrations

Minilessons link our curriculum and ask us to consider state and national standards, curriculum guides, and the students we teach. They also create the story of our teaching. We plan for students' success by engaging multilingual students in well-designed minilessons, where we convey our teaching points clearly, use visuals, provide strong demonstrations, monitor our language use, and carefully consider what we know about students' lives in order to make the curriculum relevant.

What Can This Look Like?

We can sketch a curricular plan for the year, but we cannot fully plan every unit or every minilesson without considering our students and their current interests and needs. There is a lot of teacher talk in a minilesson, and making that talk accessible is central to supporting multilingual students' writing. In the following example, I build from Ms. Rojas' third-grade unit of study on writerly life by illustrating how I incorporate what I know about several multilingual students' lives and literacies and how I weave that into my planning.

What do I currently know about my students that may inform this unit's minilessons? (See Figures 3.7 and 3.8.)

I want to make sure that in this unit, for example, I illustrate first languages as an important resource when rehearsing one's story. So I am going to ask Jorgé to tell his story in Spanish first and use him as a model for the other students. I want to build up his confidence since he often turns to everyone else before writing.

As I created the minilessons for this unit, I made a chart that addresses the four minilesson categories (see Figure 3.8). But I also made a note of how I can engage or scaffold for these particular students. This kind of planning takes some extra time, but this differentiation helps students to acclimate more quickly into the whole classroom climate. It's worth it!

Unit of Study: Writerly Life

What do I currently know that I could weave into mini-lesson in this unit of study?

<u>Writerly life</u>: Use examples children have shared recently about taking care of siblings, going to the flea market, and raising chickens.

<u>Writing Process</u> Show children how to add details by describing feelings. Share Akua's example of how she slowed down time by describing how she felt when she landed in the United States.

Things I notice in student work: Show students how telling a story in first language can may help them remember more details. Ask Jorge to model.

<u>Language focused lessons</u>: Dialogue: Demonstrate how dialogue helps readers understand characters. Illustrate how Juan described waiting at the hospital for his sister to be born and how his dialogue showed how nervous his dad was.

Figure 3.7

LESSONS ABOUT WRITERLY LIFE (the content related to this study)	LESSONS ABOUT WRITING PROCESS	THINGS THAT MY STUDENTS NEED	POSSIBLE LANGUAGE LESSONS
Labels can identify objects in your picture. (a first place to start for newcomers)	**How do writers decide what to write?** (refer to the children's hobbies or siblings)		
Writers tell stories from their everyday lives. (can refer to flea markets, church events, translating, being away from family members, moving, dance class, taking care of siblings)	**Writers revise their stories by adding more when describing their feelings.** (Ask Akira to show students how she remembered more about her trip to America when she thought about how she felt when she got off the airplane for the first time.)		**How to use students' primary language(s) as placeholders.** (Demonstrate writing and model for students that if they can't think of the word they need in English to write the word in the language they know so they can come back to it. Ask students to tell me how to say "grandparents" and model it in my own writing.)
Writers can draw stories to help them remember details. (Possible connections: Remember when Graciela told us about her baby brother being born and how small he was, like a kitten, when she held him?)	**Writers edit stories for end punctuation.** (Some students are still using periods or ignoring end punctuation. Draw their attention to texts; point out that end punctuation lets the reader know what they mean. Have students work with partners to help one another with end punctuation.)	**Approximate spellings.** (Jorgé, Javier) Model and make a chart with approximated spellings. At the end of writing time, ask children to share spellings they tried and add them to the class chart.	

Figure 3.8

(continues)

LESSONS ABOUT WRITERLY LIFE (the content related to this study)	LESSONS ABOUT WRITING PROCESS	THINGS THAT MY STUDENTS NEED	POSSIBLE LANGUAGE LESSONS
(Ask Jorgé to show his picture from the lake on the day he learned to swim. Ask him to add details and then talk about what he remembered by adding to his picture.)		Writers often write in their first language(s) and then translate because they may think and feel first in Spanish, Japanese, or Chinese. You can do this too. Then we can translate your writing into English.	Writers often write in their first language(s) and then translate because they may think and feel first in Spanish, Japanese, or Chinese. You can do this too. Then we can translate your writing into English.
Writers can tell their stories across pages. Look back at students' notebooks and look for a story that they could stretch across pages (e.g., Juan taking care of his baby sister).		**Tell your story in Spanish/Japanese** (to someone else or yourself) before writing it in English. Sometimes it helps to rehearse a story in Spanish, and then we can write it in English. (Jorgé, Juan, Graciela)	

Figure 3.8 Continued

4

The Art of Doing

After first-grade teacher Sarah Stewart finishes her minilesson about adding details to illustrations, two students carry the crate that contains the students' writing folders. The two students call students' names and children take their folders and spread throughout the room—some return to their tables and a few stay on the carpet where they sat for the minilesson, but they stretch out on their bellies and unfold their writing folders.

Sarah has six multilingual students in her room this year. Pablo, a student who speaks Spanish and whose English is developing, returns to his desk and continues to work on his picture book about the class bird, a parakeet named Tweety. He works quietly at his desk but gets up once to go look at Tweety to make sure he spelled his name correctly and to draw his beak with more detail, just as his teacher emphasized a few minutes ago.

At another table, Linda and Ariel, two girls who also speak Spanish, are sitting side by side talking while they are writing. Ariel says, "Voy a escribir sobre mi hermana." (I am going to write about my sister.) Linda giggles, "Voy a escribir sobre la maestra!" (I am going to write about the teacher.) Ariel proceeds to draw a picture of herself pushing a baby carriage and writes very slowly in English: "I walk with my sister." Linda writes: "Ms. Stewart always forgets that her glasses are on her head." Throughout the room, children are talking with peers while writing and others are working quietly. Some children are looking at books to help spell their words, others are drawing before writing. Some are writing and then drawing pictures. All are engaged in the work of writers.

Brian Cambourne (1995) calls this kind of immersion an "essential condition" of learning. According to Cambourne, we must spend time engaged in the repetitive *doing* of the thing we are learning. Independent writing time, like Pablo, Ariel, and Linda participate in each day, provides multilingual students with regular opportunities to practice, explore, study, and inquire into writing.

Many of the reasons why daily independent writing supports our monolingual students' literacy development are the same reasons that support our multilingual learners. Through independent writing, multilingual children, like their monolingual peers, have the space and time to learn writing practices, explore language(s), develop identities as writers, and make the kinds of decisions that writers must make.

The Importance of Identity and Agency

In his books, *Choice Words* and *Opening Minds*, Peter Johnston analyzes the power of teacher talk and its influence on students' perceptions of themselves and on students' academic achievement. Johnston (2012) argues that children who have a "fixed-performance frame" about themselves do not attempt or learn to solve academic problems when they are confronted with challenges, simply because they do not see themselves as capable. For example, a child who does not think she is competent at mathematics may shut down when introduced to logic problems that require her to take multiple steps to solve a math problem because she links her lack of experience to an innate quality; she makes it mean, "I am not good at math."

These children do not see themselves as capable mathematicians (identity), and this inhibits them from attempting new learning (agency). As you can imagine, this leads to a downward spiral where children may avoid more challenging learning tasks, see themselves as failures, and fail to act strategically (Johnston 2012). Teacher talk can reinforce these failure narratives when we say things like, "Joey just doesn't get math," or "Math is really hard for Joey."

In contrast to this "fixed-performance" narrative, Johnston describes a "dynamic-learning frame," wherein children are highly engaged and when learning gets tough, they dig deeper, use strategies, think about their own processes, try something new when what they know doesn't work, and seek help from others who are more experienced. In short, children who have adopted a "dynamic-learning frame" do not see their failure to learn as an inherent character flaw. Instead, they view it as part of being a learner. In learning to solve a new logic problem, these learners would ask themselves what the problem was asking them, they would think through or write steps for working through this math problem, and then try it. In short, these students understand that failure and mistakes are just par for the course when learning and integral to seeing oneself as a learner. Johnston writes:

> Building an identity means coming to see in ourselves the characteristics of particular categories (and roles) of people and developing a sense of what it feels like to be that sort of person and belong in certain social spaces. As children are involved in classroom interactions they build and try on different identities—different protagonist positions. (23)

Our classroom interactions and structures with multilingual learners should offer students opportunities to see themselves as social scientists, mathematicians, readers, and authors. Johnston continues, "If nothing else, children should leave school with a sense that if they act, and act strategically, they can accomplish their goals . . ." (29).

When teaching writers in general, and multilingual writers in particular, we must take special care in considering the kinds of curricular structures we include in our classrooms. Regularly scheduled independent writing time is essential for multilingual students in order for them to develop an awareness of their own writing practices and decisions. In essence, they become the superheroes of their own writing lives. This sense of agency is integral to their identities. They understand that although writing is not easy and presents challenges, they are capable, competent people who are able to strategically craft texts that serve their purposes.

Guiding Philosophy for Developing Independent Multilingual Writers

Johnston's (2004, 2012) research draws our attention to the nuanced, yet powerful, implications of teacher talk, which I address in detail in Chapter 5. It reminds us that we continually enact literacy practices in our classrooms that send clear messages about how literacy work is done here. If we give multilingual students grammar exercises, we are essentially telling them that form matters more than function and that writing is a set of discrete skills to master (Street 1995). But if we recognize that multilingual children need time to develop a writing identity and a sense of agency as writers, a different philosophy guides our work. Here are some guidelines to consider in helping to strengthen students' sense of agency:

1. Writers Need Time to Write

In *Time for Meaning*, Randy Bomer (1995) reminds us, "What we do with time is what we do with our lives" (2). As literacy educators, we make important decisions about how we organize the time we have with students each day, and these choices impact students' lives and their learning. When teaching multilingual writers, we must remember that writing, like all other learning that happens in our lives, takes time. Dedicating time in our literacy curriculum for the study of writing is essential if our students are going to see themselves as people who write with purpose and passion. When we commit part of our day to the study of writing (ideally between 30–45 minutes), there is a better chance that we will facilitate our students' writing identities and their literacy growth, because they will come to depend on, plan for, and think about their writing work outside of the designated writing time. This helps them approach each writing day with purpose and intention.

But it isn't just time for writing that matters. Lucy Calkins (1994) writes that creativity flourishes for writers and artists not because of an environment overloaded with stimuli, but rather through predictable structures and routines. These rituals and routines (how often, how long, and how we organize our writing time) are integral to multilingual students' independence. When writing time happens the same way every day, multilingual students know where to find what they need and how to get going because writing workshop looks and sounds the same. We want our students to know that writing begets writing, and we trust this process so much that we will not forgo this time in their day or the routines that foster their creativity.

This time does pay off. Theresa, a first-grade teacher, tells the story of Aida, a Spanish-speaking student, who greeted her at the classroom door one day declaring that she had thought of three poems on the bus that she wanted to write during writing time. Because of Theresa's steadfast commitment to independent writing time,

Aida and her classmates were thinking about writing before they even entered the classroom, which they knew nurtured and encouraged their writing identities.

Questions to Ask Yourself . . .
About Independent Writing: Time and Structure

- How many days per week do your multilingual students participate in independent writing?

- How many minutes per day do your multilingual students have for independent writing time?

- Does writing time happen at the same time each day?

- What routines and rituals do you do to prepare students for writing time? (Do you stretch before writing workshop? Do you sing?)

- What rituals and routines do you have to indicate the beginning and ending of writing time? (Do you use chimes, turn down the lights, use a word?)

- Do students have quick and easy access to writing folders, notebooks, and other tools?

---

2. Writing Is Individual and Idiosyncratic

As much as ritual and routine are important to writers, it is also important to note that these writing practices do not occur in a linear, lockstep order. Attempts to simplify a complex process are a disservice to multilingual children; anyone who has ever undertaken a writing project knows that writing can be a messy business, with lots of moving back and forth between reading, drafting, revising, rethinking, and editing. In independent writing, our students should have the opportunity to experience these writing processes at work and take notice of them.

Although writing processes and practices are similar for all children, writing development varies. Some multilingual children move quickly to more conventional forms of text, and others take more time, even when students have similar experiences with the English language (Fu 2009; Samway 2006). Students may even regress in a particular kind of writing task, such as when they are not familiar with the type of writing they are doing; when they are trying something new, such as using dialogue in a story; or even when using new writing tools (see Samway 2006, for an extensive discussion).

Knowing that writing development varies for each child and across pieces of writing means that we need to engage long-term, continual assessment of multilingual students' writing (see Appendices F and G for suggested observation and writing assessment protocols). And while we take a long-term view of writing growth, we can also support students in studying their writing lives, helping them get in touch with their individual writing habits and routines (Bomer 2011). A close examination of students' writing lives helps multilingual children construct a narrative where they are writers with particular histories, interests, and processes. There is much we can do to help multilingual students begin to understand their individual writing practices and idiosyncrasies.

TRY THIS

Ways to Support Individual Habits and Processes of Writers

Early in the year, conduct a study of writerly life where you and your students study their writing preferences. For example:

- Experiment with lighting and music in the room, asking students to think about which they prefer (bright lights, low lights, soft music, upbeat music, or quiet)

- Ask students whether they prefer to sit at a table or desk, near other people or far away from others (do they need to be alone or to talk with others?)

- Ask students to consider which writing tools they prefer: pens, markers, pencils, or computers

Have conversations with students about these experiences and record their responses on chart paper. Do this kind of study a few times a year to document how students' writing practices change.

Study writing processes as well:

- Ask children when writing feels easy and when it feels hard

- Ask multilingual children to think about which language(s) they are thinking in when they are writing and how that feels

- Ask students to notice what language(s) they write in and when

- What topics do students usually write about?

- What kinds of writing do they enjoy? (poetry, fiction, blogs, how-to, memoir, etc.)

- Do they write at home? If so, what kind of writing do they do?

Teachers usually confer during independent writing time, but it can also be very informative at times to take an ethnographer's stance and watch students for a short amount of time, recording observations without interpretations. It can feel strange to do this, but these observations can guide future minilessons, fuel discussions during sharing time, or become the subject of writing conferences.

In one third-grade classroom where I worked, I found that Amelia, a Spanish speaker, would write more when she was sitting next to other students who also spoke Spanish. She would ask her friends questions in Spanish and then write more text. Though her teacher, Ms. Carter, did not understand what Amelia was saying, she was able to see that at this point in Amelia's writing life she was more productive when she could ask her peers questions and sit near people with whom she could easily communicate. Ms. Carter didn't judge this behavior, but rather took this into account when she was conferring with Amelia; she would strategically include Amelia's peers and talk about their writing together. Amelia always talked more during her writing conferences when Ms. Carter did this.

3. Multilingual Writers Learn Best When They Forge a Connection Between Their Home Language(s) and English

When we foster students' multilingual literacies, students have a greater chance of succeeding academically (August and Shanahan 2006; Goldenberg 2008; Nieto 2010). If we go back to Johnston's "dynamic-learning frame" and students see that they have learned one (or more) languages, then they are able to see that learning another language is adding to what they already know, not replacing the language(s) they know, which are an important resource.

Independent writing time is the perfect learning context for students to write in multiple languages. When they use the language(s) they know to support their writing development, we teach children that they can use the language(s) they speak as a resource for writing (Laman and Van Sluys 2008). Though multilingual students' experiences writing in their language(s) varies, there is much we can do to foster this literacy development during independent writing time.

Inviting and encouraging children to write in the languages they know serves important academic and social functions. First, multilingual children are more likely to express complex thoughts and ideas in the languages in which they know how to write (Fu 2009; Samway 2006). Children are then more engaged in the writing processes because they are not struggling with what they want to say and, most importantly, they feel competent. Danling Fu (2009) emphasizes that when we let children write in languages their teachers cannot read, they are writing for themselves and developing writing skills for themselves—not for their teachers. In some cases, we may help students translate their writing into English, depending on the purpose and audience. We can enlist the help of community members, family members, school personnel, or the Internet to help us translate what children have written.

Some teachers have told me that this suggestion makes them uncomfortable because they are responsible for teaching their multilingual students to write in English. My response is always the same: whenever you teach something new, you make connections to something the children know and are familiar with. When we build on students' linguistic resources by asking them to write in the languages they already know, we are doing just that—taking what is known and applying it to what is new. Students' multilingual writing serves as a launching point for further teaching (Buly 2011; Fu 2009; Samway 2006). When we encourage children to use what they know, they come to see their first language(s) as an indispensable resource in acquiring additional languages and literacies.

Ways to Support Students' Multilingual Writing Practices During Independent Writing

- Invite children to write in the language(s) they know.

- Encourage children to use the languages they speak as a placeholder when they don't know the English equivalent.

- Show children what code-switching can look like. For example, some children may simply insert words subconsciously (*en* for *in*), others may be more intentional, using first languages to express an idea that they cannot yet fully express in English.

- Show students how to label drawings in multiple languages.

- Encourage children to talk in their first languages during writing time, reminding multilingual children that they can help one another with their writing.

- Make sure children have access to bilingual resources, such as bilingual picture dictionaries for younger children.

- Make a chart with cognates (words that are either the same or almost the same and have similar meanings in two languages). For example, *observe* and *observar* (Spanish) or *celebration* and *celebración*.

- Have a list of translation websites available to students, such as www.translate.google.com, www.bing.com/translator/, or www.babelfish.com for students to refer to. (Keep in mind that translations are not 100 percent accurate. Also, there is great variation within languages, depending on local dialects or the regions of the world where the language is spoken, but these sites can still be very useful places to start.)

Using a Student's First Language: Akira's Story

Akira's Initial Identity as a Writer: When Akira came to the United States from Japan in January of second grade, she was already bilingual and biliterate. She spoke Japanese and Chinese and was also able to write in both languages. But Akira was a complete newcomer to English.

Support Provided by Her Teacher: Ms. Ross gave Akira a writer's notebook, just like all the other students had, and pantomimed writing in the notebook. Ms. Ross then showed Akira a book she owned that was translated into Japanese. Ms. Ross pointed to the Japanese characters and then pointed at Akira's notebook. Akira understood and began writing in Japanese. When Ms. Ross' class studied *All About* books, Akira wrote about Japan in Japanese (see Figure 4.1A).

Akira's mother helped to translate Akira's Japanese writing into English (see Figure 4.1B).

Using Independent Writing Time to Build Skills: During the remainder of the year, Akira often wrote in Japanese first or drew pictures, which her ESL teacher then used to help her write in English (see Figure 4.2).

きせつが あります。わたしがすきな
きせつ は はるです。なぜかと
いうと そのときに 花 がさきます。
みんな おべんとうをもって こうえんに
いて そのはなを みにいくからです。

Figure 4.1A

Chapter 3: <u>Four   seasons</u>

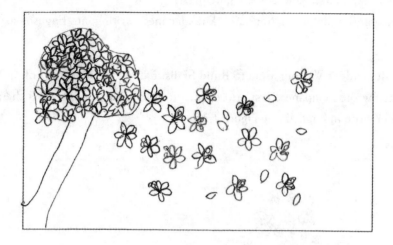

In Japan, four seasons are separated clearly.

Each season has its special beauty and events.

I like spring most, because many beautiful

flowers bloom in this season. A lot of people

would bring their lunch boxes and eat under

cherry trees when enjoying watching the pink
cherry blossom

Figure 4.1B

Figure 4.2

These early opportunities to write in her first language while learning English kept Akira engaged during school and built on the linguistic resources she already possessed. Ms. Ross fostered her students' multiple languages by making it clear that what Akira already knew in Japanese and Chinese would help her to learn English. Just one year later, in third grade, Akira wrote the following notebook entry during a memoir study (see Figure 4.3).

① My mom eats alot of spicy food. She almost eats it every day when ever I try one of the thing she eats my toung is berning. The food she eats is very spicy. I always like it when I go to sleep because my mom hug me or sing a song and read a story. After she leaves I wish I will see her very soon next morning.

Figure 4.3

76   FROM IDEAS TO WORDS

TRY THIS

Letter Writing in Primary Language(s)

Consider letter writing as a tool to help your children begin writing in their first language. When you introduce this engagement, you may have a number of multilingual students who will ask if they may write to family members in other countries. Let them! As writers, students need to consider their intended audience. If a child speaks Spanish or French or Farsi, then it makes sense that the letter is composed in that language (see Figure 4.4).

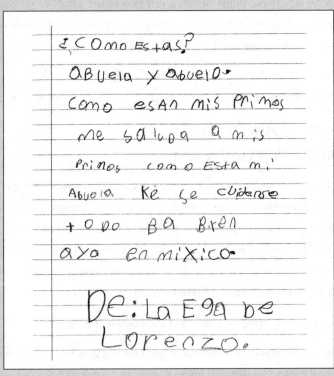

Figure 4.4

4. Multilingual Writers Need Opportunities to Write a Variety of Texts for Different Purposes and Audiences

Writing is a complex process, and the kinds of writing we do varies in terms of purpose and audience. Texts have different structures and linguistic features (Gibbons 2002). Multilingual students learn a lot about the English language and writing when they have the opportunity to read, study, and create a variety of texts across a year of workshop teaching. Through units of study, students learn about author's craft, genre, and writing processes, and they develop a repertoire of writing skills and writing practices. For example, within a year in a fifth-grade classroom, students may study feature articles, learn how to conduct interviews and surveys, study and write historical fiction, create bilingual picture books, write essays about important social issues, study poetry, and write blogs about their lives, etc. Through this yearlong curriculum, children are invited to take on the identity of someone who creates these kinds of texts and makes the kinds of writing decisions that authors make, thus expanding on the writing practices and literacy repertoires that multilingual writers will need.

Questions to Ask Yourself . . .
About Writing Curriculum

- What units of study have I planned for this year? (Do I have a balance of units that include writing process (writerly life, collecting, drafting, revising, and editing), genres (poetry, memoir, feature articles, essays, historical fiction, bilingual picture books, blogs, etc.), and times where children choose the kinds of independent writing projects they want to do? Have I left room for studies that my children express an interest in learning?

- Do my students write for a variety of audiences and purposes?

- Do my multilingual students have access to charts where we record the features of the various kinds of writing that we are studying? (For example, when studying feature articles, I have a chart with examples of interview questions, examples of facts and opinions, examples of beginnings and endings, and key phrases one may find in feature articles, etc.)

- Do my students have access to charts with key vocabulary, transitions, and other linguistic features that will help them as they construct texts?

The Act of Writing Is Being a Writer

Children's writing practices and projects give us opportunities to know our students as people living in the world, outside of school. For teachers, reading and studying students' writing provides a springboard for conversations—about moving, being bilingual, and family celebrations—as well as giving us insights into the funds of knowledge (Gonzalez, Moll, and Amanti 2005) students bring to school. Ultimately, independent writing supports students in becoming people who create and make meaning from their lives, across languages and across their lifespans. I cannot imagine time better spent.

What Can This Look Like?

By observing students during writing time and examining their writing products, we make more informed decisions. We see beyond "errors" to understand children's approximations and the sense they are making from our teaching. Below, I share my notes of one writer's notebook entry (see Figure 4.5A). Bae is a fifth-grade student who moved to the United States from Korea.

Bae was a newcomer to English. This is his first notebook entry. I used several questions from the observation form in Appendix G to analyze this entry and get a better understanding of Bae's current writing in English and to consider next steps (see Figure 4.5B).

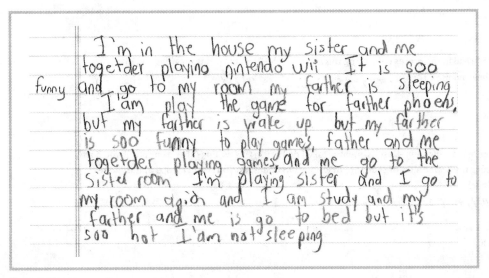

Figure 4.5A

OBSERVATION OF SINGLE WRITING PRODUCT

NAME _Bae_

NAME OF WRITING PROJECT/ NOTEBOOK ENTRY _8-19_   _N. Bentry_

INFORMATION ABOUT THE LANGUAGE (S) CHILD SPEAKS AND/OR WRITES THAT MAY INFORM MY READING

(For example, does the child write in a logographic (uses symbols) language like Chinese? Do adjectives follow nouns? Does the child write in language(s) other than English?) (remember www.omniglot.com is a useful resource for learning about features of languages)

- subject/verb/object structure which means Bae could write sentences like - Sally the ball hit.
   - Absence of marking nouns with plurals means Bae might write something like Five apple

After reading this piece of writing, what did I learn about this student that I didn't know before?
   - plays Nintendo
   - has a sister, mother, dad

What are lines, words, ideas that stood out to me in this writing that affected me as a reader that I can name for the child? "Father and me together playing games" - reminds me of Soyung Park's descriptions of family in Dear Juno

(When you said that the ocean tasted like tears, I never thought of the ocean that way before, and now I think I will always think of your writing when I get saltwater in my mouth)

Where is the child in the process of writing this piece ? (collecting, nurturing, drafting, revising, editing, a final published piece) - FiRST N. B. entry

What traces of teaching (mini-lessons/mentor texts) do I see in this writing? (For example, if you have been teaching the importance of sequence in writing directions, do you see evidence of this in the child's writing)
   - Writing from life

Figure 4.5B   Page 1

What risks do I see this writer taking in this piece of writing (writing in a new genre, about a new topic, using first language, writing more, spelling difficult words, using dialogue, etc.)?

Writing in English! Conveying meaning, and approximating English.

Do I see the student's language resources informing this writing? (Does the child write in their home language, use cognates, use first language as a place holder, code-switching, write in English with first language syntax, (i.e. The dog old chased me. etc.)

Not enough writing to know for sure.

What surface patterns do I notice in this writing (Note spelling and punctuation patterns. For example, if all words that end in tion are spelled shon, this would make an important teaching point. If the child is using dialogue, but is not yet sure how to use punctuation for dialogue, take note of this so that you can teach this to the student or the whole class if appropriate.)

What do I notice about grammatical patterns? (Is the student writing pattern sentences, statements only, complex sentences?) Again, take notice of patterns.

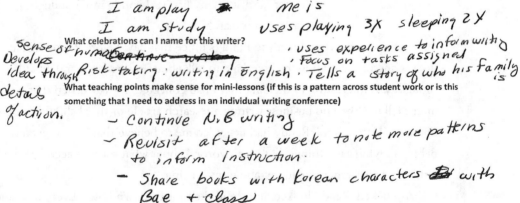

I am play
I am study   *me is*
uses playing 3X   sleeping 2X

What celebrations can I name for this writer?

Sense of humor
Develops
idea through Risk-taking : writing in English
details
of action.
• uses experience to inform writing
• Focus on tasks assigned
• Tells a story of who his family is

What teaching points make sense for mini-lessons (if this is a pattern across student work or is this something that I need to address in an individual writing conference)

— Continue N.B writing
~ Revisit after a week to note more patterns to inform Instruction.
— Share books with korean characters with Bae + class

Figure 4.5B   Page 2

5

Conferences

For years, I watched skilled teachers like Carl Anderson, Isoke Nia, and Nancy Reynolds conduct writing conferences, and I've conducted conferences with many children in my own classroom. But I had never experienced a conference as a writer until I was a graduate student at Indiana University. I was working on a research article for a class and met with my professor, Randy Bomer, to discuss my first real entrée into conducting classroom research.

I was nervous when I went to Randy's office that day. Before Randy would discuss any of my writing, he asked me to talk about my research and what I thought was interesting in the data that I had collected. I was worried that he might tell me I had no business writing a research article or that I should just give up on graduate school. Randy had never led me to believe that he was even capable of saying such things, but I was worried about what such an accomplished writer and researcher would say about my writing.

As I talked, Randy looked at me and then jotted down notes. Every now and then, Randy would stop and ask me a question, which told me that he was listening to me. After I finished talking, he asked me to talk more about a metaphor that I had used in describing my data. I told him that I saw very young children often acting as lifeboats for one another during literacy events: jumping in to help a friend write or read a difficult word. I made this comment without really thinking much about it, but Randy brought it to the forefront of our conversation and asked me to explore it more. He then recommended that it might be a useful way for me to write about my classroom observations.

When I left Randy's office that day, I was inspired to write. I felt that inside the "drafty" writing I had completed there was a kernel of good thinking that I could develop further for publication. I also finally understood what it meant to have a writing conference that carries the writer forward.

That experience also reminds me of the vulnerability we feel as writers. We all know that feeling, when trying seems like too much of a risk, where it feels safer to be invisible, or when the chance of failure feels like a complete erasure of self. Our own experiences obligate us to provide both instructional and emotional support in and through writing conferences. These two kinds of support are not different, rather they overlap. Many of our multilingual students already know vulnerability, as an outsider, as newcomers to English, when experiencing a new culture or a different instructional framework and/or school. So a writing conference is always an invitation to be recognized, inspired, and poised for the action of writing.

When I conduct professional development with classroom teachers or work with preservice teachers, they are often scared of writing conferences in general and of conferring with multilingual students in particular. They are scared that they will say the wrong thing. They worry that they may not know how to help a writer, or if they'll be able to refer to the right mentor text, or how they will communicate without a shared language. And the list of worries goes on. I always ask teachers if any of them remember a teacher sitting next to them to ask them how their writing was going. Many of us do not have memories of teachers who were interested in us or in our writing. I remind them that the first step is to remember that a conference is a conversation first. The rest of the skills will follow.

A Conversation About Writing

Writing conferences occur during independent writing time and are the ideal context for individualized instruction, understanding our students, and engaging in authentic conversations with students as writers. As Lucy Calkins (1994) reminds us, these conferences are writer-to-writer conversations, with teachers sharing their experiences as writers. Conferring with writers is always the highlight of my classroom visits because these conversations identify all the intentions that inform the words on the page. In everyday life, we talk through problems with people we trust, and in writing that authentic habit serves the same purpose. Sometimes the talk is enough for the student, and all I have to do is listen.

Unlike minilessons, where there's a momentary emphasis on teacher talk rather than child talk, conferences are more balanced, with children often talking more than we do. When we sit down to talk with a child during a conference, we want them to look forward to talking with us about their writing, so the conversation needs to be joyful and purposeful. Because some multilingual students have difficulty with extensive conversations in English, we want to make sure that our students feel a level of comfort with us, even if our exchange isn't in fluent English. Sometimes the student isn't the one who is uncertain, but rather it's the teacher who needs clarity on the student's process and intention.

Initially, conducting conferences with multilingual children can feel difficult and may even feel awkward at times, just like real conversations can. But writing conferences are rewarding, and they bring richness to our teaching that is indispensable. My goal is that by the end of this chapter you'll see how the instructional framework of a writing conference is actually a trajectory from uncertainty to action.

In this chapter, I share two essential writing conference responses that demonstrate our desire to listen to and teach from our multilingual students' strengths. In each section, I share strategies and examples of language that we may use with students that reflect these intentions. These sentence starters are not prescriptive, and they are certainly not exhaustive. Instead, they are meant as an entry into what might feel like a different way of teaching. I know that the opportunity I had to listen in on Isoke Nia's conferences with students helped me to refine my teaching and my thinking about conferences over the years. I'm hopeful that these models for writing conferences will feel helpful to you in similar ways and that they'll help you avoid the "red-pen grammarian" that can unintentionally silence your multilingual writers.

First Response: Listen Actively and Record

Because I am working toward a level of independence that allows students to trust their own voice, listening is always my foundational move. Really listening to another means giving them your full attention. In many contexts, listening may mean making eye contact and nodding. It may mean uttering an affirmative phrase. It may mean repeating what the other person said and asking them if that is what they meant. All of these actions signal listening, and our multilingual students need to know that we are indeed listening to them and that we are interested in them and what they have to say.

Conferences can feel strange when we have been used to asking questions that we know the answer to, such as, "What is the capital of Peru?" But when we ask a question like, "What did it feel like when the children teased you on the bus?" the only appropriate action is to listen and be intent on understanding. To help keep the focus on what matters, I challenge teachers NOT to instruct. This includes not teaching any spelling, editing, or grammar rules when they first begin conferring. This is especially important with multilingual children. If you are like me, this will be hard. After all, many of us know how to address editing and grammar. We know how to mark up writing. We know how to teach the difference between *to, two,* and *too*. But conferences need to be about addressing writers as storytellers first. And that involves our ears more than our pens. Some of the strategies below can help with the art of listening.

Listen for Content, not Correction

When conferring with multilingual writers, I accept their English language approximations. For example, if a child says, "Me, dad, mom goed to Wal-Mart last night," I do not correct him. Instead, I listen, knowing that the point of the conference is communication, and this sentence is easily understood. Some of the following sentences indicate what listening for content may sound like:

- What would you like help with today?

- Show me what you have done so far.

- Talk to me about something new you are trying.

- Why is this piece of writing important?

- Tell me about this writing.

Observe Before Speaking

Some students who are newcomers to English or to the classroom may not yet feel comfortable talking one-on-one during conferences. It is vital to have strategies for communicating with these children when we do not have a shared language. In these conferences, I observe quietly for a few minutes, taking notes and watching for the student's writing behaviors before I speak. Early on, I may point to something on the paper that the child is doing well, smile, and move on.

Facilitate Communication

Another strategy to implement with multilingual children in the early stages of learning English is to ask more yes/no questions. I know this seems contrary to the vision of writerly conversations that I advocate, but these kinds of questions serve as an early conversation scaffold. Children can answer me with a nod. I often talk more than the child does, pointing to their work and smiling or naming what I notice, for example:

- Is that your dog?

- Oh, I see you have five people in your picture. Who is this?

- Is that you?

- And then what happened?

- Show me a part of your writing that you like (or dislike), etc.

Go to the Children

I encourage teachers to move around the room rather than pulling children aside for conferences, because, as Larson (1999) found in her research, when teachers conduct conferences among students, other children "overhear" these conferences. You may be talking to one student, but your suggestions may well work for other writers nearby. In a video where I am conferring with a first-grade writer, one of his classmates can be seen in the background, physically leaning in and listening to the conference. When I asked the first grader to whom I was talking to turn to a new page in his writer's notebook, the student behind him (who was eavesdropping) immediately did the same thing that I had just asked her classmate to do. Children who are nearby may also chime in during a conference, offering an insight or a suggestion. Also, students can overhear us attempting to learn students' languages. It is in these kinds of conversations that we build a sense of community as writers.

Record Your Conference Notes and Your Teaching Point

It's imperative that we have some record of our teaching, partly because it is impossible to keep it all in our minds. Writing while conferring saves time and helps maintain records, but most importantly it helps you stay focused on the student with whom you are conferring. When I confer with a student, I jot down notes in a notebook with a section for each child. I include the date, what the child is working on, what the child said, and what I taught, as well as what I may look for the next time I visit the child. (See an example of my conferring notes in Figures 5.5A and 5.5B on pages 103–104.)

Facilitating Communication to Confer with Newcomers to English

Sometimes we don't conduct writing conferences with newcomers to English because we don't want to intimidate the student, or we worry that we won't know what to say. Sometimes we are uncomfortable just trying to communicate. But we are doing a disservice to multilingual children when we do not take the time to confer with them. Conferences give us the most detailed view of children's ongoing literacy learning and understanding. Also, it's worth remembering that most human communication is nonverbal, so the inability to speak Arabic, French, or Vietnamese, while inconvenient, does not prevent us from communicating with our students who are beginning to learn English.

When I first confer with a child who is a newcomer to English, I find out if the student can write in his or her first language. This is important information that will help me facilitate writing development. If the student can write, or has begun to learn to write, in his or her first language then I encourage the student to continue to do so, and I may have a conference like the one I had with Akira in her first week of school. If the student does not yet write in his or her first language, then I will observe during writing time, encouraging the student to draw first so I can support further writing in English. In the following conference, I show you what an early conference with a student who is just starting to learn English may look like and how I facilitate communication.

Akira: Second Grader, Emerging English Speaker, Fluent in Japanese and Chinese

When I first met Akira, she had just arrived from Japan and was a newcomer to English. On Akira's first day in the classroom, I sat down with her during writing time and used the conference time as an opportunity to talk with her. We began to engage in a series of back-and-forth questions and answers about how to say things. I waved my hand and said, "Hi" and wrote *Hi* in English. She then wrote "Hi" in Japanese (see Figure 5.1).

> **Tasha:** Hi, Akira. My name is Tasha. (*I point to myself and say* Tasha.) What is your name? (*I point to Akira.*)
>
> **Akira:** (very quietly) Akira.
>
> **Tasha:** This is how we write "Hi" in English. (*I write "Hi" and then wave to her.*) Can you write "Hi" in Japanese?
>
> **Akira then writes characters in Japanese.**
>
> **Tasha:** How do you say, "Hi" in Japanese?
>
> **Akira says** *Hello* **in Japanese, and I repeat after her** (Ohayō). **(She giggles.)**

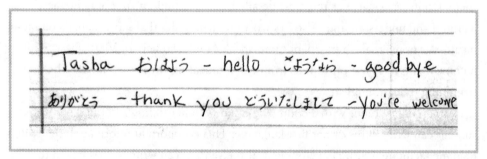

Figure 5.1

Tasha: Can you write it in Japanese?

Akira writes *Hello* **in Japanese.**

Tasha: Good-bye! (*I stand up and wave as though I am leaving. When I sit back down, I write* goodbye.)

Akira writes *good-bye* in Japanese and teaches me how to say, "Good-bye" in Japanese (Sayōnara).

This continued for *thank you* (Arigatō) and *you are welcome* (Dōitashimashite), all phrases that Akira would use in school. My goal in this conference was to see if Akira could write in Japanese. I do not write or speak Japanese, but because Akira was able to make marks that were either Japanese or that closely approximated Japanese, I knew she was comfortable writing.

I had no idea whether what Akira said to me was perfect Japanese or not, but that was not important since the goal of the conference was bigger than "getting it right." I wanted to demonstrate a genuine interest in Akira and show her that I wanted to communicate with her. I wanted her to know that her language(s) were important resources and that she could teach others in her classroom. I wanted her to get used to writing and talking to me, and I wanted to create a warm and inviting atmosphere. I wanted to give Akira more attention in those early days of school in the United States. Here are some other strategies I used in this conference:

1. I used gestures to convey meaning.

2. I repeated the Japanese words that Akira said and wrote.

3. I made sure Akira knew that she could write in Japanese while she was learning English in her new classroom.

4. I increased my wait time (up to a minute) for a response.

Using Illustrations to Scaffold Communication

I think many children, not just multilingual children, avoid writing because they don't feel confident about letter/sound relationships, especially as their peers may be growing in their writing fluency. I also think that for some multilingual students, writing in English, on top of hearing it all day and reading it all day, can just feel exhausting. When children arrive at school who are newcomers to English and do not yet write in their home languages, I most frequently turn to their illustrations and drawings as a launching point. Through these, I am able to engage children in conversations about their lives, teach storytelling, and build connections between illustrations and written words.

Carlos: First Grader, Emerging English Speaker

Carlos frequently avoided writing time. He started school in kindergarten as a newcomer to English, and at the beginning of first grade he was producing short phrases orally. While many of his peers were writing simple sentences, Carlos was still producing random strings of letters, occasionally writing words we could identify. On this day, in late August, I used Carlos' drawing to verbally scaffold his storytelling.

> **Tasha:** Hi, Carlos. What are you doing as a writer today? (*I point to his picture.*) Carlos drops his writing on the floor (*not an uncommon occurrence when I come by to confer with him*).
>
> **Tasha:** Read your writing to me.
>
> **Carlos:** (*looks at his writing*) I play Power Ranger. I play soccer. I play park. I play donkey.
>
> **Tasha:** You played with the donkey? Did you ride it?
>
> Carlos nods and smiles.
>
> **Tasha:** (*pointing to his drawing*) Wow! You were playing Power Ranger and you played soccer and you played at the park *and* you played with the donkey! Look, you also wrote, "Mexico." See it? (*point to the one word I can read*) Carlos, this is the most writing you have done. Writers write a lot, just like you did. Congratulations! Muy bien!
>
> Carlos smiles.

In this conference, I noticed that Carlos had made a detailed drawing of a park or fair in Mexico. I knew it was in Mexico because Carlos had said during the minilesson that he wanted to write about Mexico. I was thrilled that Carlos focused on his drawing and spent the entire writing time engaged—a new practice for him (see Figure 5.2).

Figure 5.2

I used the following strategies to validate his work.

1. I repeated his entire story back to him, establishing that I listened to him.

2. I noticed that he wrote a number of letters at the bottom of the page, including a
   clearly written word: Mexico.

3. I drew upon my history with him as a writer and celebrated this new growth in
   his writing.

4. I noticed that most of his writing was short, complete sentences.

5. I didn't correct any of his approximations, such as "I am playing the park," because I wanted to encourage him to talk with me and to continue writing.

6. I didn't ask Carlos to write anything more on his paper.

7. I pointed to the drawing as I retold what I heard him say.

8. I asked embedded yes/no questions.

9. In my notes, I recorded that I wanted Carlos to continue to practice telling stories from his drawings.

Use Listening for Content, Not Correction, to Teach Labeling

When we listen with an ear for the message a speaker is conveying, we turn our attention to meaning making. This kind of listening helps us teach to a student's intentions and consider one thing that may move this writer along, something that is just within this writer's grasp (Anderson 2000).

Lisa: Kindergartner, Spanish Speaker, Developing English Speaker and Writer

Labels are a great resource for multilingual writers. They can be used during read-aloud, minilessons, and shared writing, and when we conduct experiments during science time. Really, the opportunities are endless! This is an ideal time to help children learn English vocabulary, particularly when we ask them to also say these words in their first language(s), because it helps children make a connection to what they already know. Making these connections explicit for multilingual students supports their language learning (Goldenberg 2008). By listening closely to Lisa, I had the opportunity to do this kind of teaching.

> **Tasha:** What are you writing about, Lisa? (*She had drawn a car with four stick people, a road, some stoplights, and two parallel lines.*) (See Figure 5.3.)
>
> **Lisa:** My mom got sick. We went to hospital.
>
> **Tasha:** Oh no. Is she OK?
>
> **Lisa:** Yes. She came home.
>
> **Tasha:** Oh, good. I am glad. What is that? (*pointing to the two parallel lines in her drawing*)

Lisa: The thing boys and girls walk.

Tasha: How do you say that in Spanish?

Lisa: *Acera*

Tasha: Oh. In English, we call it a "sidewalk." Will you teach me how to say it in Spanish?

Lisa: *Acera*

Tasha: *Acera*

Tasha: I'll say it in English, *sidewalk*, and then you say it in English, OK?

Tasha: *Sidewalk*

Lisa: *Sidewalk*

Tasha: Lisa, you can make labels for your drawing just like Ms. Rodríguez did in her writing today. Where could you put some labels? (*Lisa points to the sidewalk and then to the people in her drawing.*) What will you label first?

Lisa: Car. (*Lisa writes* car *and then points to the sidewalk.*)

Figure 5.3

Tasha: Wow! You know how to spell *car*. Do you want to label the sidewalk?

Lisa nods.

Tasha: OK, let's say it slowly. (*We stretch out the word* sidewalk, *with Lisa saying the letters with me as she writes them.*) Lisa, look, you stretched out all the letters. When you make other drawings, you can add labels just like this.

Because conferences are layered with meaning and multiple strategies, here are some of the strategies I used in this conference to extend Lisa's learning:

1. I addressed Lisa first as a person by asking about her mother, then as a writer.

2. I asked her about the details of her drawing.

3. I asked Lisa to say a word in Spanish, and then I practiced it, reinforcing that we are all language learners.

4. I taught Lisa a word she can use immediately in her writing and that may become part of her vocabulary.

5. I asked Lisa to add a label that can support her text later, when she adds lines to her story.

6. By listening, I supported Lisa in writing a label that she wanted to try.

7. I explained to Lisa that this strategy does not just apply to this current piece of writing but to her future writing as well.

Second Response: Teach from Students' Strengths

By listening and talking to children about their experiences, their lives, and their writing, we remind students that we care about who they are and what they have to say. All of us need these reminders, and multilingual students are no different. Of course, it's not about just recognizing the student as a person, it's specifically acknowledging the work that led to the writing on the page before us and then teaching from that work.

One way to support children during writing time is to "notice and name" (Johnston 2004) what they are doing as writers. For multilingual students, this noticing and naming is essential because we're helping students to see the skills and genius in their own work. We are drawing attention to their smart writing moves and developing meta-awareness of their own writing processes. Our response answers a few implied questions from students. In the section that follows, I unpack these questions and identify some key strategies for answering them, specific to multilingual writers.

Identity: "Do you remember who I am? Do I matter to you?"

Every writing conference we have becomes part of the shared history that we create with our students. Implicit when we confer with students is a concern about whether we know our students, what we remember about them, and what they care about.

When we make our teaching point in a conference, bringing what we know about the student into our teaching raises the level of our work beyond simple strategies to complex human engagement that's tailored for the student next to us. Here are some ways I reference what I know about students:

- You are like [this writer] because you keep writing about [X], something I know you are passionate about.

- You talked about [X] in morning meeting a few days ago, and now I see it is coming up in your writer's notebook.

- Your family told me how responsible you are at home, and I saw this in your writing about [X].

- I read [X] this weekend, and it made me think about you and that you have been writing about [X].

Significance: "How is my writing talking back to the world?"

Often missing from formulaic writing instruction is a sense of significance, but writing workshop and writing conferences are steeped in meaning. Conferring with children reinforces the point that the writing work they are doing matters beyond a grade and a single reader (the teacher). In writing conferences, we have opportunities to remind students of the wider audiences for whom they are writing:

- I bet [X] is going to giggle when she reads [X].

- Who did you write this for?

- Your writing [X] made me think about [X].

- Writers like you . . . .

Extending: "How do I put that in writing?"

For multilingual students, conferences often afford teachers the time to talk about idiomatic expressions and other nuances in the English language. Although we do not want all of our conferences to focus only on the English language, some of our conferences provide timely support and specific language instruction that multilingual students may need. These conferences sometimes take the form of coaching conferences. Coaching conferences (Anderson 2000) are conferences where you are the more experienced writer, verbally extending what a writer may not yet be able to do on their own. I like to think of it as equivalent to whispering in a writer's ear; it helps move their thinking and writing forward.

In the early grades, these kinds of conferences often include stretching out sounds for young writers, helping them to "hear" the sounds that make up words. Other times, coaching conferences may help a writer do something they have never done before, such as create a scene using dialogue. In the conferences below, I act as more of an expert than I may normally do, coaching the children as they listen for sounds in words and begin to spell phonetically. As you can see from the other examples in this chapter, these are not the only kinds of conferences, but I also want to illustrate that there is a time and place where we help students with spelling, generating text, and mechanics. In addition, research shows that teaching skills within meaningful contexts support multilingual students' literacy learning (Freeman and Freeman 2001; Goldenberg 2008).

Use Mentor Texts to Note Significance

Children's literature and other published writing (student and professional) are my favorite teaching partners. Between the covers of books and the print in newspapers, blogs, and essays are texts we can use to mentor our students, texts that show them writing practices and craft that will help them grow not only as readers but also as strategic writers who study texts to inform their writing lives (Ray 1999). (See also Appendix C for more suggestions.)

In a study of bilingual writers, Kyleen Jackson's fifth-grade students studied Monica Brown as a mentor author. Kyleen carried a couple of key titles to use in conferences to suggest (and sometimes insist) that students notice, try, or emulate. Referring to mentor texts helps us to stretch students as writers by teaching specific skills and reinforcing their writing identities. Here are some sample suggestions:

- You use metaphors in your writing, just like [X].

- A poet you might want to read is [X].

- [X] writes a lot of nonfiction, like you.

- Let's see how [X] uses point of view in [her] writing and how you might too.

- I know you have been reading [X], and I can see [X] in your writing.

- This sentence makes me think of when this writer does [X]. You're both using this tool to . . .

- Remember when we talked about how writers sometimes show us what they are thinking and how we call that internal dialogue? Where is a place you might want to try that in your writing?

Inspiration: "Why should I return to my writing?"

Inherent in any writing conference is the expectation that the writer will delve back into her writing. When a writing conference is inspirational, the writer leaves the conference with more energy than when she began. The writer should feel like this writing work is worth exploring, much like I did in my writing conference with Randy.

This idea becomes important when we begin to explore the content of our conferences with multilingual learners. If all of our conferences are focused on editing and grammar, then the conference is not inspirational. It turns into a litany of all that is wrong with students' work. I have worked with many multilingual learners over the years who have been subjected to too many red pens that have crossed out and corrected verb tenses and pronouns. This often leaves students reluctant to write. When we make other observations about students' writing and their writing process, we have opportunities to build up students' resilience and inspire them to go back into their writing. Here are a few ideas:

- The topic you are talking about is important because . . . , and when you revise [X] it will . . .

- I thought the way you described [X] was original. I hadn't thought of that before, but it makes sense because . . .

- This part where you showed [X] is called [X], and writers use it for many reasons, just like you did. Are there other places you might do that again?

- Where do you want help?

Identity as a Writer: "What kind of writer am I? Am I getting better? Can I get better?"

When we notice and name students' learning, we are inherently marking students' growth and reminding them that this daily work they are engaging in is worthwhile and that we, as their teachers, see it. Naming this growth and helping student's recognize it themselves is inspiring and helps writers return to their writing with energy. This is crucial for multilingual writers. Here are some observations that can help clarify identity for writers:

- You are writing a lot.

- You are adding a lot of detail.

- You are writing much more in English than you used to.

- You told your story to [X] in Spanish first, and she noticed that it helped you write even more words on the page. Sometimes telling a story in [Spanish] first makes writing easier.

- How are you changing as a writer from the beginning of the year?

- What did you notice about yourself as a writer today?

- You wrote this whole story in Spanish! I can't wait until everyone hears it.

Recognizing Identity to Teach Bilingualism as a Writing Strength

Nowhere else in our day do we have more of an opportunity to recognize and build on a student's individual linguistic and cultural resources more than we do during writing conferences. This is where we can ask questions about children's language resources without putting them on the spot, where we demonstrate our desire to learn and understand and to know what our students know, and where we can teach strategically so that children continue to see and experience the value of speaking and writing across languages. It is especially important for students who already are literate in another language so we can help them build on that resource.

Esperanza: First Grader, Spanish Speaker, Expanding English Speaker and Writer

Several years ago, Theresa Kelly, a first-grade teacher conducted an action research project as part of her Master's program. She wanted to know what would happen if she encouraged her multilingual students to write in their home language(s). Most of her multilingual students spoke Spanish and English. In January, Theresa and her students engaged in a brief unit of study about nonfiction writing. Theresa taught her students how to interview one another, and then the students turned their interviews into books about their friends (see Figure 5.4). Esperanza, a student who spoke English and Spanish, loved to write and was very excited about asking her friend Jane questions. Since the fall, she had become increasingly interested in writing in Spanish.

Theresa: What are you writing today, Esperanza?
Esperanza: About Jane.
Theresa: What have you learned about Jane?

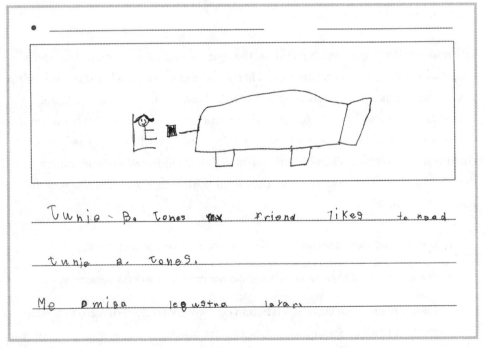

Figure 5.4

Esperanza: She likes to read. But I don't know how to write it in Spanish.

Theresa: So, you want to write it in English and Spanish?

Esperanza: Yeah, so Jane's mom can read it.

Theresa: Of course! You are thinking about your audience, the people who will read this book. Let's see what you have. "My friend likes to read." Well, how do you say that in Spanish?

Esperanza: *Mi amiga le gusta leer.*

Theresa: OK, I think I can help you with some of those words. You know how to spell *mi* and *amiga*, right?

Esperanza: Yes. (*begins to write* mi amiga)

Theresa: OK, let's ask Tasha how to write *le gusta.*

Tasha: You know the first letter for *le.*

Esperanza: L.

Tasha: *Le* is a tricky word because it makes a different sound [in Spanish] than it does in English. It has an *a* sound but it is an *e*.

Esperanza: Oh. (*writes the letter* e)

I then watched as Esperanza listened for the letter sounds in *leer,* which she approximated with "layar." In this conference, Theresa asked Esperanza what she was writing today. She also asked her what she had learned about her friend. These opening questions help guide Theresa, but then Esperanza lead the way for Theresa when she said that she wanted to write her book in English and Spanish so that Jane's mother could read her writing. This is exactly what we hope will happen in our conferences: that children will tell us exactly what they want. Other strategies Theresa used to support Esperanza:

1. Theresa reminded Esperanza that she knew how to write *Mi* and *amiga.*

2. Theresa accepted approximations and did not correct Esperanza's grammar.

3. Theresa noticed that Esperanza is becoming a writer who clearly understands audience and purposes for writing and shares that with her.

4. Theresa encouraged and facilitated multilingual writing as a norm.

Cultivating Community to Return to Writing Work

Writing can feel like lonely, tiring, and exhausting work. Writing conferences are the place where that loneliness is lessened, because writers are able to talk, think, and share. They have the opportunity to ask someone else to think with them. Our very youngest writers are often talking to one another, over each other, and even writing on top of each other's words, but as children get older this highly interactive writing shifts, and the writing conference brings it back to the social. Just the opportunity to have someone say something nice or help to solve a writing puzzle is just what a writer needs to return to the individual work that all writing entails.

Carlos: Fourth Grader, Expanding English Speaker

By fourth grade, Carlos, the student I conferred with earlier in this chapter, had grown to like writing. His fourth-grade teacher was doing a unit of study on responding to writing prompts, helping the students consider what test makers were asking and how to write thorough responses. In the following conference, I helped Carlos delve back into his writing by asking him how I could help him respond to a prompt about demonstrating love for others:

> **Tasha:** What part do you feel still needs some work, Carlos?
>
> **Carlos:** (*points to a sentence that says* I show love by kindness.) I think it needs more.
>
> **Tasha:** Carlos, you are really thinking like a reader and a writer because you know it needs something more and you aren't quite sure what to do about it. So, what are some ways that you show love?
>
> **Carlos:** When I leave to go to the bus stop I give my mom a hug and a kiss. Sometimes, if they can't finish something like taking the trash out, I will do that too. My mom really likes it that I still give her hugs and kisses.
>
> **Tasha:** I bet your mom likes that. One of my nephews went through a phase where he didn't want to give good-bye hugs and kisses to his mom, and she was really upset. I bet your family appreciates all of your help too. See, Carlos, what you said is just the kind of example your reader needs so they can understand how you show you love and care for your family. Adding what you said will make the piece better, but you already knew that. You just needed to talk first. That happens for me all the time as a writer.

Like Esperanza, Carlos identified what he wanted in a writing conference. This is a very different conference than we had when he was a first grader. Here are other strategies I used to support Carlos as a writer:

- I put Carlos in charge of the conference by asking him what kind of help he wanted.

- I listened to Carlos and demonstrated that by repeating what he said and sharing my own example.

- I asked him to talk as a rehearsal for his writing.

- I named his writing moves and validated his process and writing instincts.

A Willingness to Step into the Unknown

I think conferences give teachers a feeling of being slightly out of control because we don't know what multilingual students will say, and we may worry that we don't have the perfect response for a student. If you feel this way, I encourage you to breathe. If, at the end of a conference, you have learned a little bit more about your student and have had a conversation with them about their life and what they are doing as a writer, you are off to a good start. If you tell a student that you are so interested in what they are doing as a writer that you want to take their writing home so you can think about what you should teach them, then you have shown your student that you are a thoughtful person who contemplates your teaching.

The more you read your students' writing and the more familiar you become with your own writing process, with those of the writers you study in your classroom, and with children's literature that you share, the more strategies you will add to your repertoire. It's important to remember that any time we enter into a conversation with another person, we don't know what they might say. Teaching is scary, and it is also rewarding. You get to engage in conversations with young writers about the things that matter to them. The wonderful thing about writing conferences is that you will build up your confidence. Day after day of conferring with writers will have you looking forward to this precious time where you help your students grow, one writer at a time.

What Can This Look Like?

Documenting my writing conferences helps me keep track of the students I have talked to, what we have talked about, and what I am currently teaching. Note-taking, like writing, is highly individual. I always write during conferences, and I tend to record exactly what children say. If I don't do this I usually can't remember all the richness that was in the student talk. But I encourage you to develop your own habits for note-taking. I offer the brief notes from my fourth-grade conference with Carlos as one possibility among many (see Figures 5.5A and 5.5B). I should point out that I

What's Love got to do with my life?

Love is important because it gifes us the ability care for our mom ,and Dad. If we did not have love. we would not have a family or frineds either. we will be alone all alone. we will be Cold Because we don't have money or new Clothing. when we have. Love we will be Happy with ower family and friends and it mean's love each other. love our parintes. and I show love by Kindness. wene I leav to go to the bus Stop. I give a kiss to my mom Dad. I help my family with hard stuff they can't finish like I take out the trash out.

Figure 5.5A

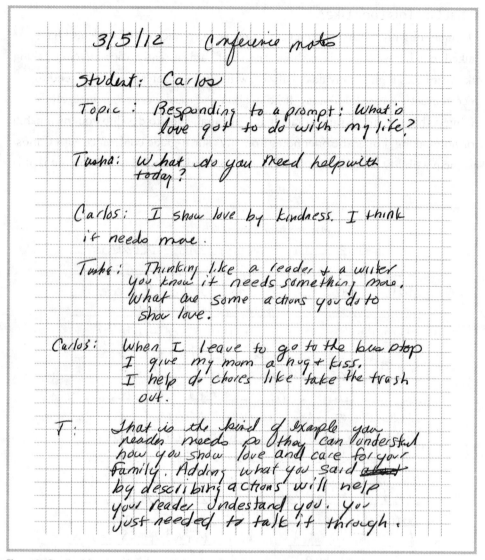

Figure 5.5B Here's how I use the information I gathered to help me decide what to do next

find it helpful when conference notes have the date, the kind of writing the student is working on, what I taught, and next steps.

I could use Carlos' example with the other children during share time or in a mini-lesson to highlight the need to read one's writing like a reader and to ask what else the student may need to do in their writing. I can ask Carlos to explain this to everyone.

Calling Out and Being Heard

6

Sharing and
Celebrating
for
Multilingual
Writers

Sarah Stewart's first graders are seated on
the classroom rug, just as they are every day during the
minilesson, but today the natural wiggly energy of first
graders is at a higher intensity. Sarah focuses them with
the reminder that, "Today is a very special day for us because we are going to share our books that we have been
writing all month. We are having our publication celebration. Whenever authors write books, they celebrate those
books by sharing them with other people."

Sarah is setting up her students for an authentic process of sharing and responding. She then reviews the procedure for today's celebration: "At 10:20, Ms.
Caine's fourth graders are coming to our classroom. Wait at your desk for your
fourth-grade partner. Your partner will come to you and then you can read your
story. After you read your story, your fourth-grade partner will write something
to you about your story (see Figure 6.1A). Then, we'll all get together and talk
about your stories and what you learned from writing them. OK? Now go back to
your seats and get ready!"

When the fourth graders arrive, their teacher, Ms. Caine, gathers them on
the class rug. She reminds them to listen closely to their first-grade partners
as well as the kinds of responses they should give to the first graders' stories:
commenting on the content of their books, what they appreciate about the

105

writing, the illustrations, etc. Then, squeezing and kneeling into the limited space by their partner's desk, each fourth grader leans in to listen as his or her first-grade partner reads.

Javier, a multilingual fourth grader, and I sit alongside Roberto, a first grader whose first language is Spanish and whose English would be considered developing. Roberto has been gaining confidence in speaking and writing English, but today we find him with his head on his desk. I ask Roberto if he is OK, but he just keeps his head down. Then I ask him in Spanish, "Qué pasó?" (*What happened?*) Roberto looks at me with tears in his eyes, but he doesn't say anything. Javier whispers to me, "I think he feels shy, Ms. Tasha." Then Javier adds, "Ms. Tasha, I remember when we did this in first grade. We wrote stories, and I wrote about the fair. Do you remember? Roberto, it was a lot of fun when I did it." Javier puts his hand on Roberto's shoulder and says, "Está bien, Roberto." (*It's okay.*) I ask Roberto if he would like me to read his story (see Figure 6.1B).

Roberto nods, and I begin to read his story aloud to Javier. When I need help reading the second page, Roberto begins to read without my help. As Roberto reads his story about a lost necklace, Javier giggles, "I know his brother, and he loses stuff all the time!" Roberto smiles.

Roberto's initial reaction to sharing is not unusual, but it's the specific context that should guide our response: a reserved first grader, Roberto, is just beginning to take risks by writing and talking in English, but the crowd of fourth graders and the excitement around the sharing overwhelm him. Sarah anticipated some of this by planning for Roberto to be partnered with Javier, someone he already knew. When I saw Roberto's reaction to sharing, I gave him just enough support to help him get started. Then Javier provided the kind of support that only peers seem able to give by telling Roberto that he did the very same thing in first grade and that it would be OK. Roberto took a risk by reading his writing aloud, gained confidence after the first reading, and then freely read his story two more times to another adult and another fourth grader. His audience members recorded their written responses (see Figure 6.1A) to his story, "The Lost Necklace," which Roberto could read later and take home to share with his family.

These experiences don't usually play out like a Hollywood blockbuster, where we see the romantic end product of success: a once-shy student passionately

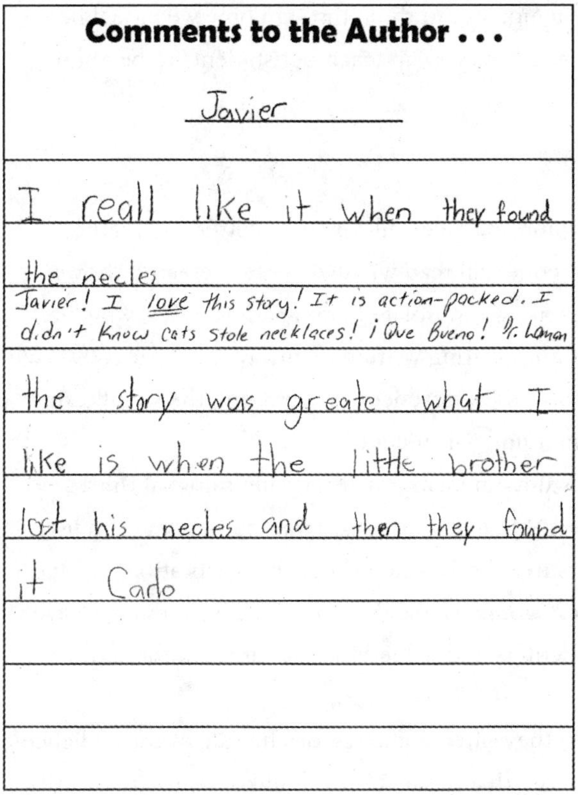

Comments to the Author . . .

Javier

I reall like it when they found
the necles

Javier! I _love_ this story! It is action-packed. I
didn't know cats stole necklaces! ¡Que Bueno! Mr. Lanan

the story was greate what I
like is when the little brother
lost his necles and then they found
it   Carlo

Figure 6.1A

Figure 6.1B

presenting to a large, rapt audience. Instead we tend to see moments of process, significant pivotal points, where a student transitions from not trying to doing. The quiet exchange between a young boy (his peer) and me (an interested adult) was loaded with significance. By sharing his learning experience, one student creates a collegial invitation to try, and taking a risk suddenly seems less threatening. It also reminds us of the essential role of community in sharing.

Audience is a concept that's significant not just to writing but to any kind of learning; we need an audience most when we feel most vulnerable. When my father taught me to ride a bike, he held the back of my seat so I knew he was right there, keeping me steady as I learned to balance. He let go as soon as I had some momentum, and then I rode down the sidewalk by myself. As we think about the power of sharing and celebrations, it's important to think about how an audience can "keep us steady" as we take a risk. Let's take a moment to think through how we model being an ideal audience for our students and how we can teach our students to be a supportive audience for their peers.

Writers Need an Audience

Whether we are sending a text, composing an email, writing a letter, or creating a fictional world, we expect that someone will read what we write. Research shows that too often multilingual children are given isolated grammar exercises, which are not helpful for learning English or for inspiring writing (Samway 2006; Fu 2009). We need to make sure we steer away from these practices by clarifying the significance and role of audience for our own multilingual students.

When Ms. Rojas did a unit of study on memoir with her multilingual third graders, she often reminded her students that first graders were going to come and listen to their memoirs. The third graders frequently asked about the celebration day and wondered whether first graders were going to like their stories. This reminder gave purpose and passion to Ms. Rojas' writers and helped focus their work throughout the unit of study.

In interviews with stage actors, they often comment on the role of the audience in a performance and about the energy that fills a theater. Unlike stage actors, writers have to hold an imagined reader or audience in their minds. Even when a writer knows who they are writing for, they still have to hold that person in their mind and envision their response. When we create time for sharing and celebrating publications, the abstract idea of audience becomes a reality and young writers experience the power of an audience's response.

It is important to teach children that audiences are active and that they have a role when they are audience members. It's also beneficial to note that there are different ways to respond in different kinds of audiences. Living in the south now for a number of years, I have grown accustomed to "call and response" in some audiences, where members in the audience immediately respond to something a speaker says— sometimes verbally and sometimes nonverbally. This kind of response, with its roots in African tradition, can be solicited from a speaker, as in, "Am I right?" and the audience responds, "Yes, you're right!" Or the audience's response can be unsolicited and spontaneous, such as when the audience responds to something the speaker has said, sometimes in expected and unexpected ways (Foster 2002; Smitherman 1985).

Geneva Smitherman describes the power of this discourse pattern in African American communities, "The interactive system embodies community rather than individuality. Emphasis is on group cohesiveness, cooperation, and the collective common good" (109). This is a powerful metaphor for sharing time and publication celebrations. Regardless of the tradition, the act of calling out to the world, whether in print or oral performance, comes from the essential human need to learn and to share new information, to be heard, and to be known. When we ask our students to share and celebrate, we are returning to that core issue of identity, but identity is something that develops over time and always within a community. When young writers discuss their writing process and share their published writing, they are essentially issuing a call for a response from their audience members, and they are positioned to receive responses in expected and unexpected ways. The power of response to urge the writer forward is a vision that we can hold as we make sharing time and celebrations integral to our writing workshops.

The Skills of Sharing and Celebrating

Sharing and celebrating require a different set of skills than participating in minilessons and writing during independent writing time; they bring writing to life and give writers a reason to write. In her book *Hidden Gems* (2011), Katherine Bomer says that we share and celebrate so we know the effect that our writing can have on our readers and so it can give us a vision of the impact we can have (164).

Sharing and celebrating also has an impact on audience members. Listening to and responding to another person's words and writing is not a passive skill. It requires our engagement with the text, calls us to form a response, and asks that we consider what we know now that we didn't know before reading or hearing the text. To be an audience member means to be responsive, and this kind of participation informs who students are as writers and as people (see Table 6.1).

We may not think there is real academic value in sharing time and planned celebrations. Katherine Bomer reminds us that teachers and students have gotten very good at the "work" part of workshop (2010, 166). Many a writing workshop runs

Authentic Publishing: A Call-and-Response Model

BECAUSE A WRITER NEEDS	AN AUDIENCE SHOULD BE
To Focus: A writer needs to read their writing, and distractions can disrupt their reading or they may lose their place.	**Attentive:** What does attentive look like and sound like? Is it looking at the writer, nodding one's head, looking down so that they can listen without visual distraction?
To Take Risks: Every time a writer shares their writing they are made vulnerable, so we want to lower anxiety as much as possible to ease students' fears.	**Supportive:** What does supporting look like? Discuss this with your students. Does it mean smiling reassuringly at a writer when they are reading? Does it mean nodding their heads? Does it mean helping when the writer gets stuck?
To Reflect: When an audience responds thoughtfully to a writer, it creates an opportunity for the writer to reflect on what they have done. During share time, this reflection may lead to revision. During celebrations, it helps the writer examine their writing decisions to this point.	**Responsive:** Audiences respond to texts in a variety of ways. Consider thoughtful compliments, constructive feedback during share times (not celebrations), personal connections, connections to other texts they have read, and questions and comments about the writer's process and product.

Table 6.1

over time without bringing the children back together again to share their thinking and learning for the day. And many a unit of study fizzles, with some children finishing the writing project and others not, with some children sharing their work along the way and others not.

It makes sense, right? We tell ourselves that the children were working really hard during independent writing, and we just ran out of time to share. We tell ourselves that this unit of study just went on way too long and we had to get going onto the next unit. But sharing and celebrations have important roles in teaching children about a writing life. Multilingual children learn and see and grow each time they share their thinking, each time they convey a message that others understand, and each time they realize that those words they are working so hard to write, in fact, do matter and have a purpose. There are essential life and academic skills embedded in the practices of sharing and celebrating student writing that make them indispensable classroom practices. Here are a few:

- A sense of courage and risk-taking

- Developing a repertoire of strategies for talking about one's writing process

- Learning to set goals and intentions for completing writing projects

- Pride in recognition of students' accomplishment; children OWN what they have done

- Authentic engagement with language

- A sense of belonging in the kind of community where we recognize and value one another's accomplishments

Sharing and Celebrations Are Writing Times

People talk about writing as an isolated activity, but only part of it is, really. Writing is a social act, in truth, but one where we go away, gather our thoughts, and then return to a larger conversation through sharing and celebrating/publishing. Sharing and celebrating are ritual acknowledgments of the audience that existed in our heads while we wrote.

Coming together each day for sharing time at the end of writing workshop (for 5–10 minutes), and then again at the end of units of study to celebrate multilingual students' writing accomplishments, reminds students why they write. When we spend time talking about students' current experiences as writers during share time and when we celebrate children's accomplishments and reflect on their writing journeys, we are actively engaging children to think about audience. We are teaching multilingual students to think about their writing processes and how to respond to their peers' writing. We are also sending clear messages to our multilingual students that their stories resonate with readers, that their writing matters, and that one piece of writing is connected to their growth as writers across a day (sharing), a week (sharing), a unit (celebration), and a year (celebration). Students need to understand that these units of time are part of their learning narrative.

I like to think of every day as a celebration when multilingual children take risks. It may be that they wrote more than they had before, worked with a new partner, tried to emulate a favorite writer, shared writing they did at home, used language in new and surprising ways, or intentionally incorporated their first language(s) into texts. Many celebrations are simply gatherings where we come together to mark the end of a current writing project. However, I agree with Katherine Bomer (2010) that, at least a few times a year, it is important to celebrate in bigger ways, which requires more time and extra planning, but that in the end is always worth it. (You'll find some ideas for bigger celebrations later in this chapter.) Regardless of whether it's a ten-minute share or a full-day celebration, there are some key understandings about writers and audience that inform our instruction and have specific ramifications for multilingual writers.

Writers Should Choose When They're Ready to Share

Learning anything means taking risks, and a new language is no different. We all have students who seem much more comfortable sharing and participating in the whole group. Although I want to make sure that multilingual children gain confidence talking in front of the group, sometimes I will give children the option to share (I give newcomers more time to adapt). I find that multilingual students often keep a low profile during share time and do not always volunteer to share, particularly if there aren't many other multilingual children in the classroom. Sometimes multilingual students may feel uncomfortable in front of their English-dominant classmates. Sometimes they may feel unsure of their English language proficiency, or they do not want to draw attention to themselves. Other times they are observing everything around them and do not feel ready to speak.

While understandable, it's our job to bring students into this regular classroom practice, over time. One way I keep track of sharing is by jotting down students' names in my notes, so that by the end of the week I know everyone has had a chance to share. This helps multilingual students become accustomed to sharing, and it reminds me to extend the invitation to share. I want students to know that sharing is just part of learning. The various strategies described below can help multilingual students prepare for sharing time.

Writers Prepare to Share: Demonstrate What Sharing Can Look Like

Just as we model writing strategies during our minilessons and conferences, we also want to model sharing strategies. During a memoir study with Ms. Rojas' third-grade students, we modeled a variety of ways to share with students. For example, one day we asked students to underline the favorite line they wrote that day. I first modeled the strategy by showing students my writing about my grandmother and underlining what I thought was my best line. Students then sat on the floor in a circle, reading over their writing before underlining and sharing their favorite lines.

Providing the demonstration and then guiding students through it helped Ms. Rojas set up her multilingual students for a successful sharing time. Choosing just one line makes the daunting task of reading aloud in front of one's peers less intimidating. It also reveals lines that are populated with meaning that can be explored further. Always consider a demonstration before sharing time in order to ensure that students understand what you are asking them to do.

In Chapter 2, I shared the importance of preparing students for storytelling, and the same is true for sharing. I often tell students what we are going to talk about during share time so they can think about and practice what they want to say. Sometimes I sit or stand next to the child and quietly coach them through sharing. I have also asked students if they would like a friend to whisper-read their writing alongside them.

Writers Prepare to Share: Giving Opportunities to Rehearse

Another useful strategy is rehearsing. For example, if you confer with a multilingual writer and want to highlight something they did in their writing, let them know that you are going to ask them to share that day. You might even practice with them if they are a student who may need a verbal rehearsal.

Ms. Rojas had worked to instill a sense of independence in Jorgé, a third grader, during writing time. Jorgé would often ask his tablemates how to spell words and would not proceed with his writing until someone looked over his work and assured him that his spelling was correct. His teacher, Ms. Rojas, noticed that this kept Jorgé from producing much text. Several weeks later, when Ms. Rojas conferred with Jorgé, she noticed that he was writing and not worrying about spelling. This was new for him. Ms. Rojas then told Jorgé that she was going to ask him to share this with his classmates that day, and they practiced together what he wanted to tell everyone about his new writing practice.

I find that after doing this several times, most children who were previously uncomfortable sharing gain more comfort and confidence, because we have developed ways of responding to one another that are supportive and encouraging rather than intimidating and scary.

Writers Don't Always Have to Talk: Displaying Writing

Because newcomers to English are often not yet comfortable speaking in front of their peers or teachers, we need to be open to ways of sharing that do not require multilingual children to speak. For example, when Sarah Stewart taught her students to think about designing book covers, she and her first graders examined some of the covers of their favorite read-aloud books. Students recognized that the illustrations and print on picture-book covers was often large enough so they could see it across the room. Sometimes illustrations wrapped around from the front of the book to the back. Other illustrations gave a clue about the contents of the book.

For sharing time, Sarah asked the children to stand up across the room and hold up their book covers so that everyone could see. Children nodded if they could see the illustration and the book title and offered suggestions when they couldn't see these text features clearly. She invited children who were comfortable sharing verbally to share what they noticed.

I first learned this strategy from Katherine Bomer when she was teaching in a K–2 classroom. When her students finished writing memoirs, Katherine invited their families and other community members to the children's celebration. She had placed a little stapled booklet beside each memoir. In small groups, Katherine had the students practice together the day before, and they were charged with helping their classmates if they got stuck at any point when reading their memoir. After the children read their memoir once, they then moved around the room and read other students' memoirs, leaving comments in the little booklets for each other.

What I love about this strategy for multilingual students is that they read their piece of writing with a supportive group of peers who are right there at the ready if something goes awry. Plus, multilingual students have the chance to read other students' writing and to respond in writing. These response booklets filled with compliments give the writer a written record to return to and read, as well as treasure.

Learning to Be Attentive: Audience Strategies

For each of these sharing strategies, consider what the audience is doing and what "attentive" looks like for your students. For example, should students look at the speaker? Should they take notes when a writer is talking? Should students nod or smile to encourage a reticent student? Should they give encouraging thumbs up? Should students write a suggestion on sticky notes for the writer to refer to? No matter what attention strategies you and your students decide on, be sure to practice them so children get a sense of what "attentive" looks, sounds, and feels like.

Because Writers Take Risks, an Audience Should Be Supportive

Risk-taking is essential to learning. Sharing in a group—trying something for the first time and sharing one's words and ideas—is risky business. Sharing time and celebrations are no different. But regular opportunities to participate in both helps writers grow accustomed to talking about their processes, sharing their words and ideas, and becoming less worried about perfection. We want students to know that the more they share and the more they try, the more they realize that they can come to depend on others to support them in their thinking and learning. Supportive audiences ease anxiety. People who nod, smile, and offer an encouraging comment give writers just the kind of support they need to move forward.

Writers Need Daily Sharing Practice to Become Confident Risk-Takers

Daily sharing time gives students practice and confidence with risk-taking. Share time also gives students a lot of practice being supportive and engaging by inviting students to engage in authentic dialogue about writing on a regular basis. Support encourages more risk-taking, which allows students to push their writing further along each day. Celebrations also create an audience who is mindful of the student's journey and growth because the other students have seen the work that the student has put into her writing over a period of shares.

Randy Bomer (2011) writes that share time ". . . can become a moment for students to name and claim their learning and progress . . ." (16). Ending each workshop with sharing time serves multiple purposes, but first and foremost it continues to contribute to multilingual students' identities as writers. During share time, multilingual writers and their peers are asked to talk about their writing processes, share what they are learning about writing, discuss their challenges, and acknowledge their goals and their accomplishments, as well as their recent learning. When multilingual students participate in conversations about their writing during share time, it provides teachers with an informal assessment, a way to check in and see the sense that students are making during minilessons and independent writing time. It also offers a chance to reflect on the larger writing curriculum and another way to teach to the student's current needs.

It's important to note that daily sharing time is not a place to have students share an entire piece of writing. If you do this, especially with older students, children will generally get fidgety, bored, or inattentive. It also limits students' chances to share. Instead, focused sharing strategies, like partnerships, allow more children to participate. Sharing time and celebrations offer another structure where students' talk about their learning makes their writing work part of an ongoing learning conversation and helps us continue to shape our curriculum.

Partnerships and Small Groups Help Writers Manage Risk

Multilingual students are learning to speak English while also learning to write in English, and the opportunity to talk about their learning supports their language learning as well as their writing development. We know that engaging with English-dominant students in meaningful contexts facilitates English language acquisition (Buly 2011; Freeman and Freeman 2007; Goldenberg 2008), and the daily opportunity to talk with classroom peers about writing provides just that kind of context. In addition, multilingual students have control over what they share because they choose what to say and to share instead of answering questions, thus lowering their inhibitions about sharing with a group.

Skillfully planned partnerships can provide multilingual students with just the right amount of support and comfort they need to participate successfully during sharing time. Pairing a newcomer to English with a student who speaks the child's first language lets the newcomer speak in the language in which they feel most comfortable during sharing time. Multilingual children who are more comfortable speaking in English may translate for their partner if they choose, but it is not required. Most of the time when I encourage these kinds of partnerships, the translation help that one student provides to another seems to happen naturally. If a student does not have a partner who has a shared language, you can also pair a student with a good friend. (See Chapter 2, for more ideas about turn-and-talk partners.)

Small audiences can also ease multilingual students' nerves. Be mindful of children's friendships and relationships. Many of the multilingual students I know also know each other outside of school. If you know that a child is close to one of your multilingual students, then pair them together. You can also ask children who they would like to have as a partner, if you teach in a school that is small enough so the children know each other.

Sometimes inviting younger classes is just the thing to do to help multilingual students share with confidence. Both Ms. Rodríguez and Ms. Rojas did this. Ms. Rodríguez, the kindergarten ESL teacher, invited the Pre-K children to hear the kindergartners' read their books. The multilingual kindergartners were confident in front of the younger children and proudly read their books aloud. Ms. Rojas, the third-grade ESOL teacher, invited the first-grade children to hear the third graders' stories. Both times, the multilingual students were positioned as more experienced writers who had written more than their audience members currently could on their own. This did a lot to build up the students' confidence and self-esteem when they shared and fueled their desire to write more in anticipation of their next writing celebration.

Beyond the Classroom: Being Aware of a Larger Audience

In writing workshops, students grow an awareness of others by developing purposes for their writing, work that extends beyond the classroom. As they gain an awareness of audience, they also gain confidence. As that growth happens, students are ready to share with larger audiences. Below I share some strategies for sharing student work with outside audiences.

Share With Other Adults

My teaching colleagues, all of whom work with multilingual children, are always interested in how their multilingual students perform in subsequent years. They often keep in touch with children's families and sometimes check in with the child and the child's current teacher. One of the celebrations I love most is when teachers ask children which teacher or person in the school building they would most like to share their published writing with. Sometimes children choose their previous year's teacher or music teacher, the school's administrative assistant, principal, or custodian. I like to introduce this celebration as the "Special Person" celebration and let the adults know why this child chose this person as the first reader of their published work.

When Matak, a second grader, wrote a poem about his home country, Sudan, he went to Theresa Kelly's room to read it to her. She cried because she knew just how far he had come since first grade, when he didn't seem to enjoy writing. You can make arrangements to have each child read their writing to their special person. Sometimes there is overlap and several children want to share with the same person. Invite that person to your classroom, and let that group of children each read to their special audience member.

Use Technology to Connect to Outside Audiences

One school district I consulted in has a telecommunications system that allows schools to connect with one another via live-feed video. A number of teachers use this technology for writing celebrations. Their children read their writing to students located in other schools in the district. This works particularly well for poetry because of its brevity. It's easy for the teachers from other districts to partner with other classrooms, and the children revel in the fact that children across town are watching them and listening to their writing! Of course, other video-conferencing tools, like Skype™, can also work well.

Megan Schmidt, a wonderful teacher who works at an international school in Colombia, created a great connection with my Master's degree students. She posted her seventh and eighth graders' writing, all of whom were multilingual Spanish and

English speakers, on Google's Drive (https://drive.google.com) site. This is a secure site, so only my students were able to see the students' writing. My university students were then assigned two memoirs to read and respond to with their comments. My students loved the opportunity to read memoirs that captured Megan's students' lives in such honest and poetic ways, and Megan's students delighted in the authentic response to their writing from university students in another country. There are multiple online forums for sharing student work. Make sure you use sites that your district has approved.

Write and Celebrate Writing in Primary Language(s)

Throughout this book, I encourage first language use, and celebrations are no different. If students have written bilingual books, invite students to read their writing in both languages. If students are literate in their first language(s) but are newcomers to English and you have invited them to write in their first language(s), encourage them to share also in the language they have written in.

Susan Ross, Kyleen Jackson, and Theresa Kelly regularly encourage their first-, second-, and fifth-grade students who know how to write in languages other than English to share their stories, books, poems, etc., with their peers. Over the years, students have shared in Chinese, Arabic, Hebrew, Portuguese, and Spanish. Monolingual English-speaking children in these teachers' classrooms learn with and from their peers and always enjoy listening to their multilingual friends read in their first language(s). This practice also sends the clear message that speaking and writing in multiple language(s) is an asset. These texts written in first language(s) also help multilingual guests to understand the stories the children have written. If children write only in their first language(s), we can then also work with other speakers of the language and use technology to help translate the texts to English if appropriate for the project.

Bringing in Family Members Can Create a More Supportive Audience

Inviting multilingual students' families and community members to writing celebrations is a powerful way to build relationships with the important people in our students' lives. Ms. Wagner and her fourth- and fifth-grade students created invitations to their writing celebration, which included blogs and short documentaries that they then sent home in Spanish and English. Several multilingual parents attended the celebration and were completely engaged by the children's presentations. They also appreciated that children had translated part of their presentation for their family members.

Celebrations are a low-anxiety context for multilingual families because they are part of an audience, they can speak to their child in their home language(s), and the teacher has the opportunity to make parents and community members feel welcome by celebrating their children's hard work.

Because Writers Need to Reflect, an Audience Should Be Responsive

While a daily time to share during writing workshop helps students develop the habit of thinking reflectively about their writing on a regular basis, reflection during a celebration allows students to turn their attention back over a longer period of time and to carefully consider their work throughout an entire project. In one study I conducted, children's reflections during celebrations were often more sophisticated than the writing the children completed, indicating that their understanding about writing was often ahead of what they could currently do in their own writing (Laman 2008). I find this is also true for multilingual writers whose final products may not fully reflect all that the child has come to know. I also find that visitors who attend celebrations are impressed with students' depth and breadth of literacy learning that is displayed through these reflections.

Making reflection integral to celebrations also serves as an informal assessment for our teaching because it lets us know what teaching ideas and writing strategies resonated most with children. When considering reflection strategies for multilingual writers, it is important to decide if our multilingual writers are more comfortable reflecting before, during, or after the celebration. It is also important for us to design multiple ways to reflect, including some oral and written strategies for learning.

Writers Need to Reflect on Their Process in Summative Ways (Celebrations)

Celebrations help bring projects to a close, and reflection ensures that students don't think of writing projects as something they can check off of a list. Rather, each project is part of the ongoing story of the writer they are becoming. Thoughtfully planned strategies for reflection bring this bigger purpose to the forefront of students' minds.

Make Charts with Questions for Celebration Reflection

As always, it is helpful to provide visual cues for multilingual writers. For students who are reading in English, write questions that you want them to think about. If possible, also write questions in children's first languages in order to facilitate their reflection. Some possible questions to ask at the end of any unit of study include:

1. What have you learned about poetry, memoir, punctuation, etc.? (Use the focus of the unit of study to guide you.)

2. What did you used to think about (poetry, memoir, fiction, etc.)? What do you think about it now?

3. Show us one part of your writing that you really like. Why do you like this part?

4. What was something you did that was new for you?

5. What (books, writers, articles, poems, etc.) did you read that inspired your writing?

6. Show us a place where you used another language in your writing. Why did you decide to do this?

7. What part of this writing project was hard for you? What part felt easy?

8. What do you want your reader to know about this published piece of writing?

9. How have you changed as a writer since you started this project?

10. What part of this writing project was really exciting, challenging, or surprising?

11. What would you teach others about this genre?

12. What do you hope your readers understand about this publication?

13. What would you do differently if you were to write (a feature article, essay, pamphlet, etc.) again?

These questions can be adapted to support students with varying degrees of English language proficiency. For newcomers to English, I most frequently ask them to show their favorite page or to share their thinking in their first language, whichever feels most comfortable for them. Choosing one or two questions is sufficient for a celebration reflection. For multilingual writers, asking students the reflection questions prior to the celebration so they have time to think about their oral response is often helpful. It is also helpful to ask students to write their responses so you have a written record of their reflection and so they can then read their response during the celebration reflection.

Strategies for Reflection During Celebration

Writers Prepare for Reflection: Making Lists and Drawing Responses

Asking someone to take a reflective stance on his or her learning is a big task. Teaching students to make lists about what they have learned can help them prepare for celebration because it gives them an outline for ideas they want to share. In addition, writing often begets more writing, and so it is for reflection. Regularly looking back on one's learning and talking and writing about it may generate more insights. Students can also draw a response for their reflection. Asking children to draw what they learned or what they remember is another powerful way for students to express themselves nonverbally.

Writers Can Reflect in Partnerships and Small Groups

Asking multilingual writers to talk to one another and reflect within a small group or partnership reduces anxiety, just as it does in sharing and celebrating. Students are not overwhelmed by the large group, and they have more time to explore their thinking and their talk. They are also able to use their primary language(s) if they need to.

An Audience Doesn't Need to Talk to Be Responsive

Graffiti boards (Short, Harste, and Burke 1996) are large pieces of paper on which children may draw or write their responses. For celebrations, we can ask children to use this large sheet of paper for their reflection, resulting in a display for visitors and for the hallway. This visual form of reflection creates a safe context for multilingual students, who may not feel comfortable talking to a large group of visitors. Ms. Wagner, a fourth- and fifth-grade teacher, used a graffiti board for her students to write what they learned from their participation in a literacy and technology project, which she then used as a backdrop during their technology and literacy celebration.

Celebrations Teach Readers How to Respond to Writing

Learning to respond to writing as a fellow reader and writer is a skill that we develop over a lifetime. Celebrations offer multilingual students opportunities to engage in academic discourse as they learn to talk about what they appreciate in other people's writing, what craft moves children have made, and to read like writers (Ray 1999). Responding also helps students consider what they are learning from a writer or a text and how this writing changes how they view the world. It also puts them in a conversation with an author's ideas. In addition, through students' comments and conversations, teachers can see what they have learned about reading and writing. For example, when Kyleen Jackson's fifth-grade students studied poetry they read poets such as Langston Hughes. Some children tried to emulate Hughes' use of African American language in their writing. Kyleen then asked children which poets seemed to influence each student's writing.

She also had some students read their poetry in their first language. Then she asked, "If you don't speak the poet's language, listen and think about how the sounds of the poem make you feel." When children shared their writing during the celebration, Frank, a student who spoke Spanish and English said, "I like John's poem because he sounds like Mr. Langston Hughes. I can tell he read his poetry." Another student noticed how Mariella wrote part of her poem in Portuguese. "I don't know what the words say, but it sounds like music when she reads it."

Documenting Celebrations Helps Writers Hold onto Their Learning

Most parents and guardians work during the school day so attending a child's writing celebration is not always an option. Every parent I know appreciates when their children's work is documented. There are many ways to accommodate family. You can record students during class celebrations and burn the video onto a CD to give to parents, or you can upload the video to a secure website for parents to access at their convenience. You can photograph students during the celebration and send the photos home with a copy of the student's writing. Other teachers I know make class anthologies and send these home with the children. I'm sure that you can think of lots of creative ways to share students' writing so that their families can see the results of lots of time and effort on their child's part.

Audit Trails of Celebrations

Creating audit trails during a unit of study creates a visual marker of the learning journey we engage in with students (Vasquez 2004). For example, take photographs of students while they are immersed in reading poetry at the beginning of a unit of study. Hang those photos at the beginning of the audit trail, then put up quotes from students regarding what they notice about poetry and their experience as poets. Continue by adding the covers of mentor texts, making lists of minilessons, hanging copies of students' notebook entries, and writing quotes from reflections during share time. Ending the audit trail with photos from the celebration and quotes from the children and visitors is a powerful way to show the timeline of multilingual students' participation and their learning. Ms. Brice, a former teacher of multi-age multilingual students, used audit trails regularly to document students' learning journeys. These delighted visitors and provided visual support for her young learners when they talked about what they had been doing in class. The trails were also completed on celebration day, adding yet another visual marker of students' learning journeys.

Opportunities to Celebrate Writers' Work and Growth: Ideas for Small-Scale Celebrations

When I was growing up, we didn't have lavish birthday parties held at pizza parlors or amusement parks. Instead, my mom would make our favorite dinner (mine was fried chicken and mashed potatoes) and our favorite cake (Italian wedding cake). Then my mom, stepfather, siblings, and stepsiblings would sing "Happy Birthday" (off-key), and we usually had a gift or two to open. These were small, intimate family affairs filled with love and, with a little planning, were fairly simple for my mother and stepfather to pull off. That is what most of our writing celebrations will be—small events that mark the important occasions of students finishing their work. The following ideas are suggestions for simple, small-scale but significant ways to celebrate multilingual students' writing.

Writers and Audiences Can Be in Charge of Celebration Decisions

When Sarah Stewart started writing workshops several years ago, she began the habit of asking her first graders how they would like to mark the end of their poetry unit of study (see Figure 6.2A).

Figure 6.2A

Figure 6.2B

She was sensitive to children's sensibilities and their ideas of what constitutes fun. The children decided they wanted to first recite Eloise Greenfield's (1986) poem *Things,* followed by a class poem they wrote (see Figure 6.2B). Then they wanted to each read their poem aloud to the whole class. Afterward, they wanted a few celebration centers set up, which included some poetry games (like poetry magnets, where they could create poems), a snack center, and a poetry listening center.

The children wanted to end the celebration with a cheer that their student teacher had taught them, which went something like, "Peel bananas, peel, peel bananas," and ended with, "Go, bananas, go, go bananas!" with lots of children jumping up and down and waving their hands in the air.

Putting the children in charge of the celebration like Sarah did take the stress off her, motivated the children to finish, and, most of all, let them own their celebrations. There were no outside guests for this celebration, just classroom friends sharing and enjoying their writing and having some fun.

Writers Can Extend Their Writing Through Visual and Performance Art

Although most of our celebrations will be small, there are times where we may want to "go big." Sometimes we may plan a surprise birthday party or a getaway or an extra nice dinner for an anniversary. The same is true for writing celebrations. Sometimes it is exhilarating to plan something extra special to celebrate the end of a unit of study.

Over the past few years, I have learned a lot from Susan Adamson, director of the Indiana Partnership for Young Writers, and my art colleagues, Dr. Karen Heid and Mr. Thompson, an elementary art teacher, and I have had the opportunity to engage in large-scale art and writing projects. Throughout this book, I talk about the importance of sketching and illustrating for multilingual writers. But these projects taught multilingual writers to move back and forth between creating visual art, participating in performance art, and writing. Engaging in each of these processes helped children extend their writing. These collaborations with classroom teachers and arts-based educators resulted in large-scale projects that impacted multilingual students' learning.

Poetry Mosaic Garden

This school-wide celebration involved months of planning and preparation among teachers, university faculty, administrators, community members, and the school district. At Market Elementary School (pseudonym), the teachers decided to study poetry because it works so well across the curriculum and across grade levels. For example, the fifth grade linked poetry to the Harlem Renaissance. The teachers also recognized that poetry is a powerful genre for multilingual students because of its brevity, its opportunity for multilingual children to use their first language(s) in powerful ways, the option to study poetry across cultures, and the likelihood that all children could participate (Flint and Laman 2012).

A guest poet did a presentation for the entire school and talked about his writing process. Beginning in January, all of the children studied mosaics in art class with Mr. Thompson and Dr. Heid and then created mosaic tiles that reflected their poems. The children then wrote their poems on ceramic tiles that were fired in a kiln. During spring break, the school district had the entire front of the school dug up. All of the children's tiles were laid in the ground and surrounded by new cement, and a bench was built, as well as a fountain. Children worked on the bench and the fountain after school and during art class. Community members also worked on the bench over several weekends.

For the day of the celebration, Dr. Heid hot glued the children's poems onto wooden boards and hung them on the schoolyard fence to create an outdoor display of the children's writing. Children enjoyed ice cream, which the PTA provided, as they strolled through the outdoor "gallery" reading one another's poems. More than 500 people, including parents, grandparents, and other community members attended the celebration. Children and visitors read the poems that hung on the fence, sought out their mosaic tiles in the sidewalk, and delighted in the transformed school entrance that had become a mosaic garden.

During a school-wide assembly, the principal asked the children how many children had written poems and made mosaics, and every child from the pre-kindergarten four-year-olds to the graduating fifth graders proudly raised their hands. The children ultimately took home the tiles with their poems on them, but the mosaics forever transformed the front of the school building, making a beautiful addition to the school's community.

When I conducted interviews with multilingual children following this celebration, Matak, a second grader said, "Before this, I didn't know I had poems inside me." Esmerelda said, "The poem and my tile is my favorite. When I see the tile, I think of my abuela, and when I gave my poem to my abuela, she cried."

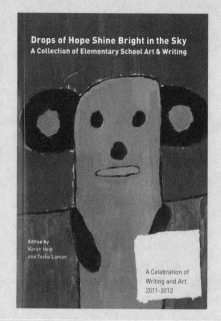

Drops of Hope Shine Bright in the Sky
A Collection of Elementary School Art & Writing

Edited by
Karen Heid
and Tasha Laman

A Celebration of
Writing and Art
2011-2012

Celebration of Literacy and the Arts

Two years later, we undertook another large-scale celebration. Dr. Heid and I worked with every grade-level teacher, asking what they would study in the fall in writing workshop and in their curriculum. Collaboratively, we planned projects with the teachers that would also include working with artists in residence. For example, prekindergarten students were learning to tell stories from their drawings, so the teachers thought that working with a dancer would help children bring their stories to life, as well as give multilingual students confidence in presenting.

First-grade teachers wanted their students to become more skilled at sharing their writing aloud. They worked with a theater arts major, who helped these young writers learn to perform for a large audience through props, as well as speaking to large crowds. Second graders studied Faith Ringgold as a mentor author and artist, worked with a quilter, and created beautiful quilt squares with poetry written in the borders. Third graders wrote with a poet in residence, and fourth graders worked with a painter and a dancer. Marius Valdes, a graphic designer and professor, worked with fifth graders who created "Secret Species"™ from clay and wrote fantasy stories about these creatures.

In December, all of the children in the school shared their writing, artwork, and performance art at a school- and community-wide celebration of the arts and literacy. The children's writing and artwork was hung in the hallway. In the spring, all the artwork and writing was scanned, and Marius and his graphic design students created

a stunning collection of the children's artwork and writing, which each child received. This project brought visual art, performance art, and writing together, allowing multilingual children to make meaning in multiple ways and to express themselves across modalities. The visual and performance art enhanced children's writing, helping them to express themselves in more detail, as well as experience the power of expression without language that is made possible through the arts.

The Pay Off

These two large-scale projects took a small army of people to pull off, and there were times when teachers, administrators, and university faculty were living it that we really wondered whether it was worth it. But when we saw the children standing on stage performing their writing, showing off their exquisite artwork, pointing out their tiles in the sidewalk, clutching their beautiful books filled with their own writing and artwork, and heard families rave about the children's writing and their performances, our collective exhaustion disappeared because all of those extra hours did make a difference.

Some ways to bring these kinds of large-scale projects to life include looking for community members who have skills that can help you plan a school-wide project and celebration. Enlist the help of the related arts teachers in your school. Our music and art teachers were instrumental in helping to pull off both of these large-scale celebrations because they had experience with coordinating school-wide performances and art installations. You can also look for state and local grants that support education and the arts. Both of these projects were made possible by cobbling together money from state and university grants, monies from the PTA, the school district, and from the local neighborhood association.

You may read this and think "I can't do that," but no one is asking you to replicate these projects. Rather, I share these to show how much potential there is; you just have to choose a scale that feels manageable to you. None of us could have done this project alone. For me, it is inspiring how so many different groups can come together around the common goal of offering children an enriching experience that celebrates their learning.

What Can This Look Like?

On the next page I share some brief planning notes (see Figure 6.3) I made to help third graders prepare to share a memoir celebration with an audience.

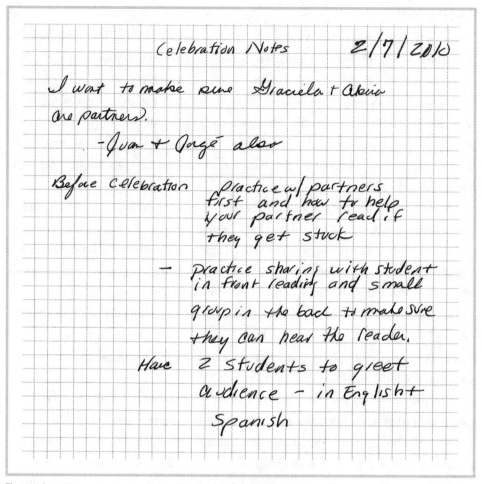

Figure 6.3

Share and Get Celebrating!

Multilingual students need opportunities to share their thinking, their learning, and their processes and to celebrate their accomplishments. Sharing and celebrating, like writing, are social acts and serve as important spaces for reflection and response. Multilingual students reflect on their purposes for writing, their thinking behind their decision making, and their writing challenges during sharing time. They do this in partnerships and whole groups.

We establish the kind of classroom environment that values rough-draft thinking and sharing, because these approximations are part and parcel of creating an entire text. Responding to texts teaches writers to consider other perspectives, to enter into a conversation with an author, and to learn from others. Finally, the response that multilingual writers get from their audience fuels their purpose for future projects. It reminds writers that at the end of each writing project there are readers waiting to read and respond to their thinking, as well as to recognize and celebrate the writer.

7

Being and Becoming Multilingual Writers

Independence, resilience, risk-taking, persever-ance, stamina . . . these are traits we want our students to cultivate and, as literacy teachers, we want them to be contextualized in students' growth as writers. But actual student writing tells just part of the story of a student's growth. Katie Wood Ray (2004) reminds us that even though student writing can feel small at times (not many words on the page) that the actual "work" is big because students are participating in the kinds of writing processes and practices that all writers engage in and that, over time and with many opportunities to practice and to engage in meaningful instruction, the actual writing can become "big" also. Learning is not just doing well but being able to reflect on what one does well. We can get students to keep moving forward by offering curriculum that invites consistent growth and contin-ued reflection. But that planning can never be removed from students' experiences and their perspectives.

In this final chapter, I feature Akira and Graciela, two third-grade girls, and one fourth-grade boy, Javier, who share their writing histories inside and outside of school. Akira moved to the United States in second grade and was a newcomer to English. Graciela and Javier's schooling experiences are similar to the majority of multilingual children in the United States, because they are growing up in homes and communities where they speak Spanish every day but for whom all formal education has taken place in English (Suárez-Orozco, Suárez-Orozco and Todorova 2008).

The children's own words add another layer to classroom notes and observations and give us insider perspectives to their thinking. All three of the children attend ESL classes during a portion of their school day. They each share their early memories of learning English and talk about their writing experiences and their growth over time. I, too, reflect on what I notice, and I name the deliberate teaching moves their teachers made in order to support their writing development. Then I share the next steps I would consider to reach and teach each writer.

My hope is that this will help you to consider where your multilingual students' current writing is and how you might move them forward with your teaching. I end the chapter by reflecting on what else we may consider when intentionally building schools and learning communities where children's cultural and linguistic resources inspire new opportunities for being and becoming multilingual.

Akira, Third Grader

- Speaks Japanese, Chinese, and English

- Writes multiple-page entries in her notebook

- Is a Drama and Dance Club member

- Is the only child in a single-parent household

- Has family in China and Japan

Akira Reflects on Her Growth

Akira: *[When she first started school in the United States]* Some words I know, but it was kind of hard to speak English at that time. When I was in Japan, I learn a little English. But when I came to America I just hear English every day and I could understand a little bit, but I couldn't say anything. I didn't really talk that much. Some of those words I know, and then when I listen to more English the more I knew and it got easier. Now I say a lot. When I listened to it, it just got easier.

[Akira reflects on the first piece of writing she completed in the United States. See Figure 7.1.] We were writing about things we like. I remember that I draw things, foods I like in Japan. I like seaweed, sushi, and rice and there's a biscuit that I drew right there in Japan that is soggy that I like. And green tea ice cream is right there that is my favorite, but it is hard to find in America. I also wrote about springtime. After I draw the pictures then I wrote in Japanese, and my mom helped me write in English. *(See Figures 7.2A and 7.2B.)*

[Akira describes how her writing has changed over time] Well I still write in Japanese and Chinese. I go to Japanese school every weekend and we write the characters and we take tests, and I still write Chinese too. It's different with English because English is alphabet and Japanese and Chinese are characters. Writing is different for me now. When I first came to America when I write in English, I had to think in Japanese first, and when I stay here for a while now when I write in Japanese, I think in Japanese, and when I write in English I think in English. Now I can read long books in English. I am reading the third Harry Potter, and I write long stories now. I like to write fiction stories. *(See Figure 7.3.)*

Figure 7.1

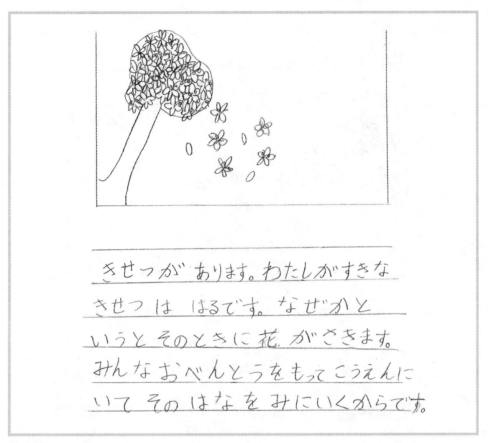

きせつが あります。わたしがすきな
きせつ は はるです。なぜかと
いうと そのときに花 がさきます。
みんな おべんとうをもって こうえんに
いて その はな を みにいくからです。

Figure 7.2A

Akira's Identity as a Writer: Traveling Across Languages

In one academic year, Akira began to read and write in English with a level of confidence that impressed her teachers and her peers. Akira's experience offers a contrast to other children's experiences where their language(s) are barred from classrooms and playgrounds (Reyes 2011). Instead Akira's experience offers us strategies and a vision for what we can do when we do not speak the same language(s) that our students do. In many ways, Akira's experience represents an ideal situation for learning English as a new language. Because Akira learned to read and write in Japanese and Chinese first, she was poised to learn English (Freeman and Freeman 2001, Fu 2009, Samway 2006).

Chapter 3: _Four   Seasons_

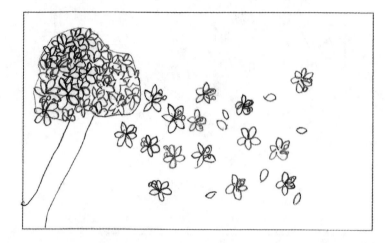

In Japan, four seasons are separated clearly.

Each season has its special beauty and events.

I like spring most, because many beautiful

flowers bloom in this season. A lot of people

would bring their lunch boxes and eat under

cherry trees when enjoying watching the pink
cherry blossom

Figure 7.2B

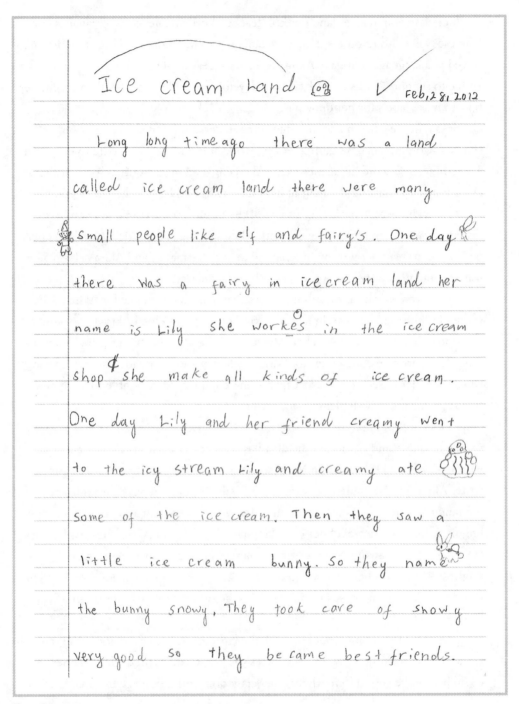

Ice cream land 😊 ✓ Feb, 28, 2012

Long long time ago there was a land
called ice cream land there were many
small people like elf and fairy's. One day
there was a fairy in ice cream land her
name is Lily she workes in the ice cream
shop she make all kinds of ice cream.
One day Lily and her friend creamy went
to the icy stream Lily and creamy ate
some of the ice cream. Then they saw a
little ice cream bunny. So they named
the bunny snowy, They took care of snowy
very good so they became best friends.

Figure 7.3

Her classroom teacher and her ESL teacher, both unable to speak Japanese or Chinese, were also resourceful, first encouraging Akira to draw. These early drawings served as a language that gave Akira's teachers access to her thinking and served as an entrée to support Akira's English writing development. Her teachers then taught her how to make labels for her drawings.

Susan, her teacher, made sure that Akira understood that she could—and should—write in Japanese during writing workshop time. Asking Akira to draw and expecting her to write in Japanese kept Akira engaged in the writing work of the classroom, and enlisting the help of her mother showed her teachers how complex Akira's thinking was. Even though some of the English translations were approximated, it gave Susan plenty to work with when helping Akira write. Akira's teachers invited her to read her writing in Japanese to her classmates, and Akira's classmates listened intently and asked her to teach them Japanese.

These were significant teaching moves that made a difference for Akira as she started her third-grade year. In fact, this kind of support helped Akira to construct the kind of learning narrative where she learned that difficult things grow easier over time. This narrative contributes to Akira's resiliency and to her ideas about learning, which help her to see herself as a capable and confident learner, able to learn new things in the midst of challenges (Johnston 2011).

Akira's multilingual identity was intact as she described the places where she speaks Japanese and Chinese. She also has an identity as an English speaker and writer. As Fu (2009) learned in her research of multilingual students learning to write, Akira was ". . . able to express [her] daily life experiences through written languages because [she] was required to write every day and [was] given the linguistic freedom to travel between languages" (71). And Akira did travel across languages, first drawing, then writing in Japanese, and, over time, writing in English. Akira's teachers encouraged her language flexibility because they understood that Akira's Japanese and Chinese literacy skills would support her as she learned English.

A year after entering school in the United States, Akira talked about the similarities and differences between the languages she knows and writes. Her experience could have gone very differently had her classroom and ESL teachers forced her to write and speak only in English. It would have limited the amount of text that she could produce and, because her English vocabulary was limited, the complexity of her thoughts would not come across in her writing.

What I Notice About Akira's Writing

Akira's teachers clearly moved Akira forward in her English writing skills. In this notebook entry (see Figures 7.4A and 7.4B), Akira wrote a narrative in English regarding her experiences.

Akira's English literacy skills continued to improve with so many opportunities to write. She does not include drawings in her notebook entries anymore, unless her teachers ask her to try sketching, or as in this entry, her teacher taught her how to use a timeline when writing about memories.

Akira now speaks and writes enough English that her words alone convey her message. She writes about things that are significant to her, which has clearly grown out of the writing experiences her teachers offered her each and every day. Her narrative structure moves from a clear beginning to an end, she uses the past tense consistently in this entry, and we can see English approximations (*drinked, that*). The approximations are expected and do not worry her teachers because the purpose of Akira's notebook is to get her writing ideas onto paper that can later be shaped and reshaped into a final writing project.

What Comes Next for This Writer?

When I envision next steps in teaching Akira, I would continue to encourage her to keep a writer's notebook. She is also poised to spend more time with longer projects, which would also support her academic language development and her content knowledge. As she and her classmates head into the upper elementary grades, I would engage Akira in units of inquiry, such as historical fiction and feature articles, where writers conduct research before and during writing. In addition to these more guided inquiries, I would make sure that Akira (and her peers) have the opportunity to choose more and more independent writing projects across the school year in order to continue to foster her sense of agency, including invitations to write bilingual texts.

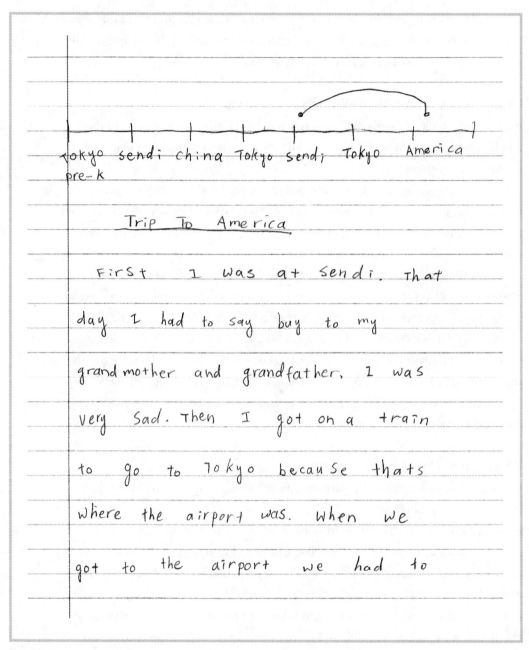

tokyo sendi china Tokyo sendi Tokyo America
pre-k

Trip To America

First   I   was   at   Sendi.   That

day   I   had   to   say   buy   to   my

grandmother   and   grandfather.   I   was

very   Sad.   Then   I   got   on a   train

to   go   to   Tokyo   because   thats

where   the   airport   was.   When   we

got   to   the   airport   we   had   to

Figure 7.4A

wait a long time to get on
the airplain to America. I was
very exited when I got on the
airplain. It took a long time
to get to America. Sometimes I
was bord. Sometimes I was sleepy.
But still I wanted to see my new
house. When we got to America we
went on another airplain to get
to columbia. The airplain was smaller.
We drinked some juce on the
airplain. I was very happy when I
got to columbia.

Figure 7.4B

Graciela, Third Grader

- Oldest child, has two younger sisters and a baby brother

- Helps her first-grade sister with her homework

- Helps mom with the baby and cooking meals

- Plays with Akira on the playground

- Writes about her life in her notebook

Graciela Reflects on Her Growth

Graciela began to learn English when she started preschool. When I asked her about her early memories of school, Graciela said:

Graciela: [*Graciela remembers kindergarten*] I don't remember much. I do remember that I did have paper, and Ms. Ward gave me this book to write in, and I wrote a lot of words in it and now I try to read it and I say, "What is this saying?" I can't read it now because we didn't know how to write, and then we grew up and we started learning how to write a little bit and now in third grade, we write a lot.

[*Graciela reflects on learning to write in English and Spanish*] I learned [to read and write] in English first; I didn't know how to write in Spanish. We always speak Spanish at home, but I didn't write in Spanish. But then when I was in first grade, I really wanted to write in Spanish. I'm learning to write more Spanish words now because my mom and dad show me because last time I was doing it by myself and no one was helping me. So, I wrote some Spanish words, and my dad said, "You wrote all of them right." I felt happy because I never know how to write in Spanish. Now, my mom and dad are teaching me to write in Spanish because I really want to. I made two cards for my mom and I wrote them in Spanish because she reads Spanish. You pronounce the words really different like /e/ in Spanish sounds like /a/ in English. Since I take a lot of English, I talk a little bit in Spanish and I say some words wrong now. My baby sister talks a lot of Spanish and says a lot of Spanish. I'm trying to do a lot of Spanish because my mama said if I talk a lot of English and not Spanish, I'll never know a lot of Spanish.

Graciela's Identity as a Writer: Striving to Be Bilingual

Graciela entered kindergarten speaking Spanish but unable to read or write in Spanish. Graciela has clearly cared about writing in Spanish for some time now. She reports that her parents both read and write in Spanish, so even though Graciela wasn't formally taught to read or write in Spanish before she started school in the United States, she was exposed to her parents' literacy practices.

Graciela has a growing awareness of her multilingual identity. Comments like, "Since I take a lot of English, I talk a little bit in Spanish and I say some words wrong now," also reflect the tenuous nature of her Spanish literacies and her deep desire to learn to read and write Spanish. Graciela's tenacity, her urge to learn Spanish, and her concern over forgetting words demonstrates an awareness of what she wants and how she engages the people she knows and trusts most to teach her.

Just as Graciela recalled, in first grade she was interested in writing in Spanish and English, but she wasn't sure if she was allowed to. Her first-grade teacher, Sarah Stewart, recalled going outside on Earth Day and telling the children to write what they noticed about their outdoor environment. Graciela asked Sarah, "What's that word for *el viento*?" Sarah does not speak Spanish and didn't know that *el viento* means *the wind* in English. Since they were outside, away from any resources that Sarah could use to look up the word, she encouraged Graciela to write the word in Spanish (see Figure 7.5).

Sarah said that Graciela seemed hesitant at first, wanting to ensure that it was OK with Sarah. Sarah remembered, "I never told Graciela that she couldn't write in Spanish, but her response to me made it clear that I also had not encouraged it either." In subsequent years, Sarah was more intentional in demonstrating how her multilingual students could write words in their first language(s) as placeholders and also to strategically use multiple languages in their writing.

This early and explicit invitation from her first-grade teacher was significant. Graciela recognized the importance of communicating in Spanish, both with her family and in her community. In school, Graciela is encouraged to use Spanish as a placeholder when writing. In addition, she participates in conversations about the value of learning languages other than English, she is permitted to speak Spanish with her classmates during independent work time, and she has access to classroom libraries with bilingual books that she can take home to share with her family. All

the SKY 's For Vinto and the

hae 's r lering uP

Figure 7.5

of these things matter in Graciela's literate life because she understands, through many language conversations with her parents, teachers, and peers, that reading and writing multiple languages has many benefits and can offer her social, academic, and economic opportunities that could be integral to her future endeavors.

What I Notice About Graciela's Writing

In this third-grade notebook entry (see Figure 7.6), Graciela has clearly grown from her early days as a writer who was sometimes hesitant to put words on the page. Graciela has learned that she has all she needs for a writing life—a life. She describes the routines and rituals of cooking, dancing, and singing that are woven into her days. Graciela's sense of being an integral part of her family also comes through. Here, she offers her teachers a view of her life, complete with caring adults and siblings. She also shares her language practices when she describes how she helps her mother with English when she needs it, just as her mother helps her. This reciprocity, and

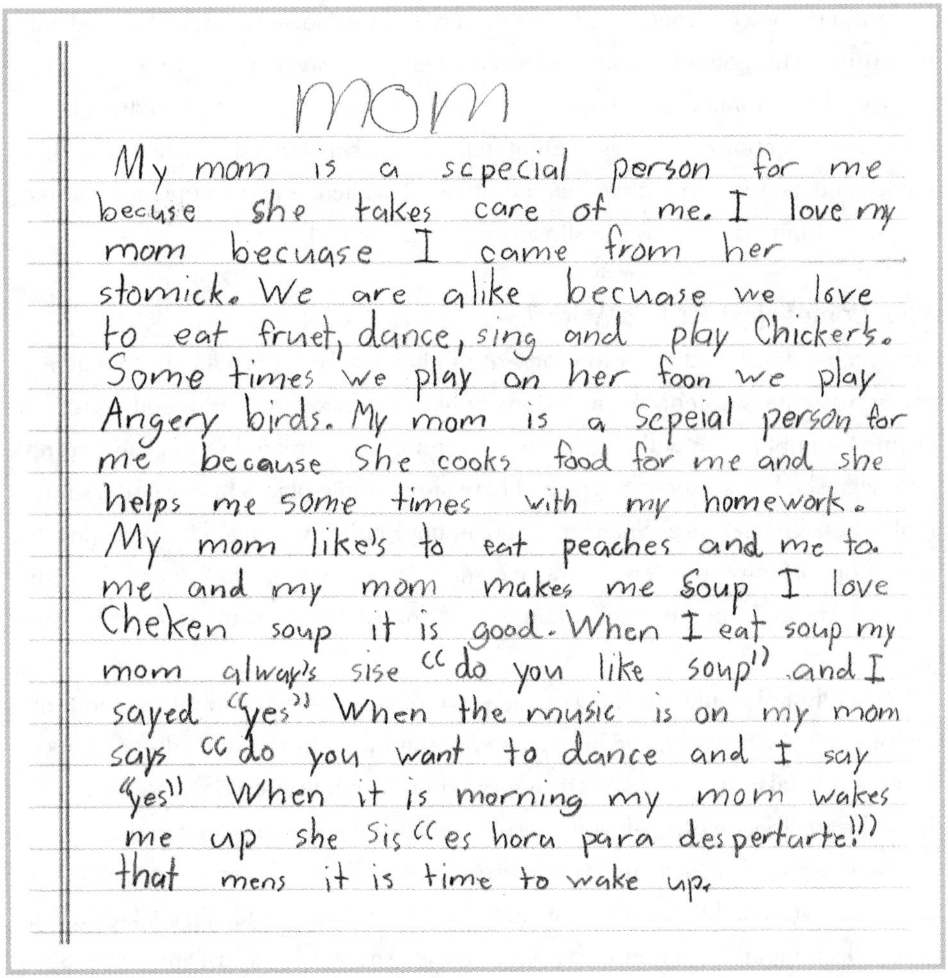

mom

My mom is a scpecial person for me becuse she takes care of me. I love my mom becuase I came from her stomick. We are alike becuase we love to eat fruet, dance, sing and play Chickers. Some times we play on her foon we play Angery birds. My mom is a Scpeial person for me because She cooks food for me and she helps me some times with my homework. My mom like's to eat peaches and me to. me and my mom makes me Soup I love Cheken soup it is good. When I eat soup my mom alway's sise "do you like soup" and I sayed "yes" When the music is on my mom says "do you want to dance and I say "yes" When it is morning my mom wakes me up she Sis "es hora para despertarte!" that mens it is time to wake up.

Figure 7.6

Graciela's agency as a writer—taking up what matters most to her—reveals the teaching that has happened over the years.

Some may read this notebook entry and notice Graciela's use of *for* when she writes "my mom is a special person for me . . ." but it makes sense because in Spanish Graciela would say, "para mí," which means *for me.* You may also notice some of her misspellings and incorrect verb tenses, etc. Graciela's teachers know that she sometimes worries about getting her writing "right," so they encourage fluency before convention. They can then help her to nurture her seed ideas, draft, revise, and edit her writing. This notebook entry reflects the beginning stage of that process. As her teachers moved through a memoir study, Graciela drafted, revised, and edited her work for conventions as well as content, but her teachers helped Graciela keep these important details in perspective, reminding her that there is always time for editing but that her important ideas can slip away.

What Comes Next for This Writer?

Graciela has developed a passion for writing. Because she is producing so much text in her writer's notebook, intentionally helping Graciela to draft and revise her writing for publication will give her opportunities to compare her English writing with what she knows about Spanish. There are multiple places in her writer's notebook where Graciela uses Spanish syntax in her English writing. This provides the perfect opportunity to teach contrastive analysis, comparing English and Spanish, so Graciela can deepen her understanding of English, while at the same time learning more about Spanish.

In addition, I would encourage Graciela to publish more writing throughout the school year, which would give her many opportunities to revise and edit her work; the more she takes her pieces of writing through the publication process, the more she will learn about writing. I would also introduce Graciela to more bilingual authors and texts that she can use as touchstone texts, where she can intentionally try the craft moves that bilingual authors make. And, finally, I would engage Graciela in more reflections and inquiries into how and when she speaks, reads, and writes Spanish, as well as the similarities and differences she notices between her Spanish and English metacognition. Raising these levels of meta-awareness will support Graciela in continuing to grow and use her multiple literacies in strategic ways.

Javier: Fourth Grader

- Helps younger children with homework
- Reads Percy Jackson books
- Plays soccer

- Is an only child and lives with his mother

- Likes to write poetry

Javier Reflects on His Growth

Javier: [*After showing him samples of his writing from first grade and second grade*] My handwriting gets better. I remember I was drawing in kindergarten and the beginning of first grade. This is my dad, me, my cousin. I remember this. I think it was on my birthday (*see Figure 7.7*). I like the one where I put my cousin Walter [in it when he] came to visit and I remember him. He has his hair sticking up too. I guess all the boys in my family have it. He came, and I was happy to see him, then he went and I was sad, but I keep telling him to come and visit, but he said it is a little bit far away. I used to write and I liked to write, but I drew pictures more. Sometimes

Figure 7.7

when the teacher was talking I was just drawing. I remember too when we had the little chicks. I wrote about them, and I remember when I wrote about soccer, and you know my friend Casey? I drew a picture of me and him playing basketball. I remember heart maps in second grade (*see Figure 7.8*) and my reading buddy, and I remember the poem where I wrote 'I hate rain.' I still have that. When my mom saw my heart map, it made her kind of happy and she kept it.

[*Talking about writing outside of school*] I do have a journal at home. It is kind of like a diary. I write about what I think about like with my dad not here, how I miss my fam-

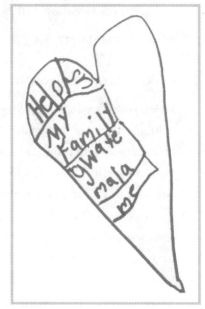

Figure 7.8

ily. It is kind of sad because my grandma died when my mom was a baby. And my other grandma died last year, and I never knew her. I write about those kinds of things. Sometimes I write about kids that are born here and how they can get visas. That's what I heard. I don't know if it is true.

[*I asked Javier if he knows how to write in Spanish*] Yes. I learned from my mom. Even though she only went to school for three years, she was always writing and I told her I wanted to write in Spanish then she started teaching me. Sometimes I write in Spanish in my diary, but sometimes I get confused because most of the time I write in English. Sometimes I misspell stuff. Sometimes I am forgetting a little bit of Spanish like how to say 'city' in Spanish. And a long time ago, I was kind of confused and I said the word "faira" but then I learned to say 'la feria' for fair. I have three languages. I speak English, Spanish and there is another one. My mom and grandpa call it 'dialecto.' I only understand a little bit of it. My grandpa speaks it the most. In the language my grandpa speaks they have different kinds of letters. I wrote a word once, but it looked weird. When I write I think in English except when I am home then I think in

Spanish. It feels kind of good to write in English because once I start writing I really can't stop. My mom says she wants to learn English too. She said "Come on teach me," and I say "It is kind of hard to teach you." My mom doesn't know English so like if the toilet gets flooded and she tells me to just write two sentences for the landlord, but I write two pages. I always have to speak English for her like there is a store close to us called Rocky's Pizza. She understands English well but she just can't speak it.

Javier's Identity as a Writer: Meaning Maker

Of all the students I have interviewed over the years, Javier has the most rich and detailed memory of his writing life. He clearly recalls the writing work he did in first and second grade. His illustrations capture more than he was able to write at the time. His first-grade teacher, Theresa, taught the children how to make detailed drawings. Javier did, so much so that three years later he recalls the details of the stories behind his drawings. His teacher also taught him how to label the drawings and encouraged him to write words in English and in Spanish, which he did in several drawings, writing *gato* for *cat* and *mi mama* for *my mother*.

After meeting with Javier, I went back to my files and found each piece of writing he described: the drawing he described where he was playing basketball with his friend Casey and the poem about rain from second grade (see below). But Javier's writing life extends beyond school. He uses writing to think and reflect on his life, to contemplate how hard it is to be separated from his family members. And he also uses writing to get real-world work done. He writes long notes to the landlord explaining problems, and he translates for his mother when she needs his help. He is continually moving and communicating across languages.

I don't like rain.
You don't get to
Go outside.
I felt sad.
I want to play outside.
My mom told me.
Don't worry.

But when it stopped
I felt happy.
It is sunny.
A boy came to me
He said can I
Play outside?
Yes!
We played ball
Until the sun went to bed.

What I Notice About Javier's Writing

Javier's teachers have instilled a love of writing in him. Each year, Javier has had writing teachers who engaged him in a writing curriculum where he was able to write about important topics and across a wide variety of genres. His poem has a strong image at the end: *Until the sun went to bed.*

What strikes me most about Javier as a writer is the fact that he has crafted a writing life that his teachers may not know about, where he writes to reflect, to think, and for real purposes, like writing notes to the landlord. Translating and paraphrasing are sophisticated skills that Javier is learning at a very young age, and these literacy practices support and serve his family (Orellana and Reynolds 2008). They remind us how smart, resourceful, responsible, and, most of all, how integral Javier and his literacy practices are to his family. Like Graciela, Javier is aware of his Spanish language skills and is concerned about getting confused when speaking Spanish.

What Comes Next for This Writer?

Several lines of thinking occur to me when I think about furthering Javier's literacy learning. It seems important that we explicitly show Javier how his translation and paraphrasing skills can also help him in school when summarizing texts, paraphrasing directions, and considering vocabulary words (Orellana and Reynolds 2008). Elevating this skill for Javier (and for his classmates) supports his multilingual identity and helps him see that the languages he knows really do matter.

Though there is not a direct transfer from home literacies to school literacies, Orellana and Reynolds (2008) remind us that these skills could be "leveraged" in school for students like Akira, Graciela, and Javier, because they are often ignored or even unknown. Javier has such a strong memory for his writing experiences that I would build more intentional reflections into the writing workshop for him, asking him to explain his thinking to his peers, to recall his process, and to share his learning journey. Because Javier spends time writing about his family and how he feels about being far away from them, I would help Javier find memoirs that he can identify with. Then I would help him turn some of his diary-like writing into more formal products, such as memoir.

I also don't want to ignore Javier's comment about immigration, because it reminds us that children are often aware of the world around them. In this case, Javier has shared a question he has about immigration. These kinds of questions offer us the chance to collectively discuss and inquire into topics that affect our students, our communities, and us. I could implement a unit of study where Javier and his peers work collaboratively to study important social issues, conduct research, and decide the most appropriate way to write for social impact (Bomer and Bomer 2001).

I am not suggesting that we make children or their families more vulnerable than many of them already are, but Javier's words remind me that the world is often on children's minds and we need to make space to talk through and write about the issues that matter to them.

An Invitation to Go Further

Listening to Akira, Graciela, and Javier's words about their writing gives us a broader view of their literacy journeys and offers us a counter-narrative where their lives and their literacies are not lacking. They all enjoy writing, take risks in their learning, and know that writing is integral to their lives. Their stories inspire me because even though their homeroom language arts teachers did not speak their languages, these students' multilingual experiences and identities were welcomed and not squelched. All three children talk about their learning and how they have changed over time. They talk about how much their teachers helped them grow. These are such important parts of developing the stance of lifelong learning.

At the same time, I am worried. Graciela and Javier express very real concerns about sometimes forgetting Spanish or about being unsure how to write words. Implicitly, Graciela and Javier understand that forgetting one's language is scary, and what one loses is more than a vocabulary but a sense of self. Language is on their minds, and it matters so much to all three children that they pursue their learning outside of school, with their families and in their communities.

These students make me think about what else we could do to ensure they are able to meet their educational goals. These reflections are not critiques of their experiences to date, because their hard-working teachers have done so much to support them. In fact, I credit their teachers for these students' passion for learning and their willingness to talk so openly about their languages and literacy learning. I am inspired to think of other, more intentional opportunities that we can offer students to foster their multilingual literacies:

- What if there were after-school clubs for students to learn to read, write, and create texts in Spanish, Chinese, Laotian, Sudanese, French, Japanese, etc.?

- What if we held family literacy nights, where multilingual families taught other families and teachers about various language(s), cultures, and countries?

- What if there were language courses offered to parents who wanted to learn English?

- What if we collaborated with local organizations to provide adult literacy classes for parents who were interested in furthering their own education?

- What if there were bilingual book clubs for students and families to participate in?

What I've offered in this book are models and invitations for ways to support multilingual writers. I know that with conversations, planning, and further study, we can help to create the kind of world where multilingual children don't give up who they are in order to learn to read and write English. Instead, they learn that their multilingual lives are integral to being and becoming strategic writers. Most importantly, multilingual children learn to bring their ideas and words to the page and to help shape their world and ours.

List of Multicultural and Multilingual Poetry and Songs

Poetry

Alarcón, Francisco X. 2005. *From the Bellybutton of the Moon: And Other Summer Poems / Del Ombligo de la Luna: Y Otros Poemas de Verano*. New York: Lee & Low Books Inc.

Angelou, Maya. 2003. *My Painted House, My Friendly Chicken, and Me*. New York: Crown Books for Young Readers.

Benjamin, Floella. 1995. *Skip Across the Ocean: Nursery Rhymes from Around the World*. London: Frances Lincoln Books.

Johnston, Tony. 2003. *The Ancestors Are Singing*. New York: Farrar, Straus and Giroux.

Kobayashi, Issa. 2007. *Today and Today*. New York: Scholastic.

Lowe, Ayana. 2008. *Come and Play: Children of Our World Having Fun*. New York: Bloomsbury USA.

Myers, Walter Dean. 1996. *Brown Angels: An Album of Pictures and Verse*. New York: First Harper Trophy Books.

———. 2008. *Jazz*. New York: Holiday House.

Nye, Naomi Shihab. 2005. *19 Varieties of Gazelle: Poems of the Middle East*. New York: Greenwillow Books.

———. 2002. *The Flag of Childhood: Poems from the Middle East*. New York: Simon & Schuster.

Swann, Bryan. 1998. *The House with No Door: African Riddle-Poems*. New York: Harcourt.

Various authors. 2009. *Poesía a la luna*. Madrid, Spain: Luis Vives Editorial.

Wong, Janet S. 2007. *Night Garden: Poems from the World of Dreams*. New York: Aladdin.

Songs

Becker, Helaine. 2011. *Juba This, Juba That*. Plattsburg, NY: Tundra Books.

Delacre, Lulu. 1992. *Arroz con leche: canciones y ritmos populares de América Latina: Popular Songs and Rhymes from Latin America*. New York: Scholastic.

Kimmelman, Leslie. 2008. *Everybody Bonjours!* New York: Knopf Books for Young Readers.

Leventhal, Debra. 1994. *What Is Your Language?* New York: Scholastic.

Orozco, Jose-Luis. 1999. *De Colores and Other Latin American Folksongs for Children*. New York: Puffin Books.

Reiser, Lynn. 1998. *Tortillas and Lullabies/Tortillas y cancioncitas*. New York: HarperCollins.

APPENDIX B

Family Survey for

_____

(Student's name)

What do you want me to know about your child?

What does your child like to do when he/she is not at school?

What would you like me to do this year as your child's teacher?

What would you like your child to learn this year?

Would you like to visit the classroom this year and teach the children about the language(s) you speak?

Would you like to help children read or write in their home language(s)?

What language(s) do you speak at home?

Would you like to visit the class and talk about your profession, hobbies, or your home country?

APPENDIX C

List of Multicultural and Multilingual Children's Books

Non-Fiction

Saunders-Smith, G. 2003. *La luz del Sol / Sunshine*. North Mankato, MN: Capstone Press.

Trumbauer, L. 2006. Â¿Que es un insecto? / *What Is an Insect? (Yellow Umbrella Books: Science Bilingual) (Spanish Edition)*. North Mankato, MN: Capstone Press.

Saunders-Smith, G. 2003. *La Lluvia / Rain*. North Mankato, MN: Pebble Books.

Fiction

Retana, M. L. 2009. *Dawn till Dusk / De la aurora al crepúsculo (English and Spanish Edition)*. Charleston, SC: BookSurge Publishing.

Hayes, J. 2006. *La Llorona / The Weeping Woman (English and Spanish Edition)*. El Paso, TX: Cinco Puntos Press.

Hayes, J. 2010. *Dance, Nana, Dance / Baila, Nana, Baila: Cuban Folktales in English and Spanish (English and Spanish Edition)*. El Paso, TX: Cinco Puntos Press.

Hayes, J. 2011. *Juan Verdades: The Man Who Couldn't Tell a Lie / El hombre que no sabia mentir (English and Spanish Edition)*. El Paso, TX: Cinco Puntos Press.

Hembrook, D., and K. Heling. 2007. *I Wish I Had Glasses Like Rosa / Quisiera tener lentes como Rosa (Bilingual English/Spanish)*. McHenry, IL: Raven Tree Press.

Crouch, A. M. 2011. *The Gnomes of Knot-Hole Manor Bilingual Chinese English*. Seattle, WA: CreateSpace.

Lemus, E. F. 2011. *Sebastian's Marimba (Bilingual English-Spanish) (English and Spanish Edition)*. San Diego, CA: Odiseas Centroamericanas.

Avelino, K. 2009. *No Ka Wai O Ka Puna Hou / The Water of Ka Puna Hou: A Bilingual Hawaiian Story*. Honolulu, HI: Kamehameha Schools.

Interest Inventory for

_____

(Student's name)

What do you like to do?

Do you have any hobbies? (Do you like to cook, play soccer, ride a bike? Read? Read comic books? Play video games?)

What language(s) do you speak?

What could you teach someone else?

What do you want to learn this year?

How can I help you learn this year?

157

Tell me about a time you learned something new. Who taught you? How did they teach you?

What is your favorite book?

What is your favorite band/song/video game/television show?

(For younger children) Draw a picture of three things you like to do.

(For older students) Who has been your favorite teacher so far? Why?

List of Grant Resources for Educators

The following four websites provide up-to-date grant information to fund classroom libraries and other school projects:

www.grants4teachers.com: This website provides advice about writing effective grants and has a search engine that allows you to look for grant resources within your state.

http://grantwrangler.com: This site is updated biweekly to provide you with current school and teacher grants.

http://teacherscount.org/teacher/grants.shtml: This site provides a range of grant resources that are available across the curriculum.

www.grantsalert.com: This website offers extensive information regarding funding sources from foundations, businesses, and government grants. Due dates and criteria are easy to identify.

The following grants (listed on www.grantsalert.com) may be particularly helpful in supporting innovative projects in the multilingual classroom:

1. **ING Unsung Heroes (www.grantsalert.com/grants/foundations/194):** This grant funds innovative and creative teacher projects that positively influence students, up to $25,000.

2. **Teacher Development Grants (www.grantsalert.com/grants/foundations/220):** This grant from the McCarthey Dressman Education Foundation provides up to $10,000 for innovative projects that include students' reflections regarding the project.

3. **National Book Foundation (www.nationalbook.org/innovations_in_reading.html):** The National Book Foundation offers a yearly prize for Innovations in Reading. Check out the website for most recent awardees and how they are reaching and teaching readers in promising ways.

APPENDIX F

Observing Students During Writing

1. Who is this student? What are some things I need to remember about this student? (if the student is new, has never been in writing workshop, is able to read and write in language(s) other than English)

2. What am I observing about the student's writing process?

   a. What does the child do during independent writing time? Remember to write only what you see, without any judgment or interpretation (e.g., Child is sitting next to another child, picks up pencil, walks over to trash can, walks back to desk rather than writing, note something like "avoids writing"). Signs of Independence and Agency: What writing strategies/ behaviors do you see the child implementing? (getting started, rereading the writing, talking with peers, etc., using a mentor text, teaching someone else, where does the child choose to sit?)

   b. What language resources do you observe the child using? (word walls, peers, individual lists, mentor texts, speaking in language(s) other than English, using a bilingual dictionary, or other resources)

Post-Observation Reflection

Reread your notes from your observation and consider the following questions as you think about turning your observations into teaching:

1. What did you learn about this child through observation that you didn't know before? (For example, one year, I was concerned about a student who seemed to avoid writing until I noticed that he was surrounded by children for whom writing seemed very easy; they produced lots of text, long stories, and they were all English-dominant. No one near Carlos spoke Spanish, he did not have anyone he felt he could ask a question, and his teacher and I hadn't noticed

because most other times Carlos seemed to talk a lot—even with English-dominant kids. But writing was an altogether different experience for him. Carlos was slow to write because he thought he couldn't write, simply because he couldn't write as quickly as his table mates.)

2. What behaviors did I observe that seem to support this writer's identity and agency? For example, does this writer know where materials are? Does she have a plan for getting started? Does she look at her friends' writing during writing time? (Remember that writing is individual and idiosyncratic, so your students' writing behaviors will not all be the same, and there are many ways to be a productive writer.) Does the student know what to do when she is done with a piece (get started on another project, turn it in for feedback, meet with a partner)? Why do you see these behaviors as helpful?

3. What behaviors did I observe that may not support this writer's identity and agency? (For example, going to the restroom four times in 10 minutes isn't going to help this writer get his work done. Nor is saying things like, "I don't have anything to write," or "I don't know how to write." Playing with a toy that is tucked in a pocket, teasing a tablemate, looking out the window during writing time, or walking to the word wall for each letter of a word is not very efficient). Why do you see these behaviors as inhibiting student's writing identity and agency?

4. What teaching points could I address in a conference about writing process with this writer, based on observations?

   a. Some strategies for keeping tools organized

   b. How to use sticky notes to write word wall words

   c. How to reread your writing before getting started

   d. How to write a note to yourself about what you plan to do the next day

   e. How to find a place to write where you feel productive

   f. Yesterday I heard you say, "I don't have anything to write." It feels that way sometimes for me too. Let's look at the heart map you made at the beginning of the year to see if we can make a plan for some upcoming writing topics so you don't feel that way.

5. What are teaching points I could address in a minilesson about writing process, based on a pattern I notice in my observations of multiple students?

   a. I noticed that we have different ways of getting started, and I want to share some of them with you because you might want to try them. For example, Farina rereads her writing from yesterday, Selena and Audra talk to each other before they start, Arielle writes a note to herself at the end of each writing time to remind herself what to do today. (Have a chart with each strategy illustrated for the students.) Turn and tell your neighbor how you get started. (Add strategies to the chart.) When you write today, you can try one of these strategies—or a different one—and we will talk about it at share time. (Notice, I did not say anything about observations of *process* that may not be productive. However, you could do a minilesson about distractions and emphasize that writing takes concentration. You could share stories about your own avoidance behaviors. For example, if my phone is near me, I tend to check it more than I need to. Sometimes you might have toys in your pocket that you are saving for recess, but it can be hard to resist them during writing time. Let's think of a place to put them where they won't distract us too much from our work.)

   b. Yesterday, I heard several students say, "I'm done!" And I realized that we need to talk about what to do when you are done. Remember that you can ask a friend for a conference, you can look over the checklist before you turn your work in, and then you can get started on your next project.

   c. Yesterday, Marisol and Juanita were speaking Spanish and writing some words in Spanish. When I asked them about it they said that speaking Spanish before they wrote and even writing in Spanish helped them think about what they wanted to write and it felt easier to write in Spanish first. That is such a helpful strategy for some writers. You may want to try that today and see what happens. (You could ask English-dominant children to think in a language they are studying in school and how it might feel to write in Spanish so that they get a sense of how writing in English feels so much more natural. Point out that it is the same feeling someone may have when they first think in the language(s) they know and are learning to write in a new language (English).

Observation of a Single Writing Product

Name: _____

Title of Writing Project/
Notebook Entry: _____

Information about the language(s) the child speaks and/or writes that may inform my reading. (For example, does the child write in a logographic language (using symbols) like Chinese? Do adjectives follow nouns? Does the child write in language(s) other than English?) (Remember that www.omniglot.com is a useful resource for learning about features of languages.)

After reading this piece of writing, what did I learn about this student that I didn't know before?

What lines, words, or ideas stood out to me in this writing that affected me as a reader that I can name for the child? (When you wrote that the "ocean tasted like tears," I had never thought of the ocean that way before, and now I will think of your writing when I get saltwater in my mouth.)

Where is the child in the process of writing this piece (collecting, nurturing, drafting, revising, editing, the final published piece)?

What traces of teaching (minilessons/mentor texts) do I see in this writing? (For example, if you have been teaching the importance of sequence in writing directions, do you see evidence of this in the child's writing?)

What risks do I see this writer taking in this piece of writing? (For example, is the student writing in a new genre, about a new topic, using first language, writing more, spelling difficult words, using dialogue, etc.?)

Do I see the student's language resources informing this writing? (Does the child write in his home language, use cognates, use first language as a placeholder, use code-switching, write in English with first-language syntax, e.g., The dog old chased me?)

What surface patterns do I notice in this writing? (Note spelling and punctuation patterns. For example, if all words that end in *tion* are spelled *shon*, this would make an important teaching point. If the child is using dialogue but is not yet sure how to use punctuation for dialogue, take note of this so you can teach this to the student or the whole class, if appropriate.)

What do I notice about grammatical patterns? (Is the student writing pattern sentences, statements only, complex sentences? Again, take notice of patterns.)

What celebrations can I name for this writer?

What teaching points make sense for minilessons? (Is this a pattern across other students' work, or is this something I need to address in an individual writing conference?)

APPENDIX H

Observation of Growth Over Time

Student's Name: _____

Dates of Writing Samples: _____

Topic/Content	SAMPLE #1	SAMPLE #2	SAMPLE #3
What does this writer understand about process? (e.g., got started, finished, shows revision, etc.)			
What evidence of teaching do I see in these samples?			
What language resources does this student use?			
What surface structure features are a strength/challenge?			
What grammatical patterns do I notice?			

What strengths do I see in these three pieces?

What future teaching is just within this student's grasp?

Questions I have for other teachers, community members, or professional resources that may help me:

References

Akhavan, N. 2006. *Help! My Kids Don't All Speak English: How to Set Up a Language Work-shop in Your Linguistically Diverse Classroom.* Portsmouth, NH: Heinemann.

Allen, J. 2007. *Creating Welcoming Schools: A Practical Guide to Home-School Partnerships with Diverse Families.* New York: Teachers College Record.

Allen, J. 2010. *Literacy in the Welcoming Classroom.* New York: Teachers College Press.

Allen, J., V. Fabregas, K. H. Hankins, G. Hull, L. Labbo, H. P. Lawson, et al. 2002. "PhOLKS Lore: Learning from Photographs, Families, and Children." *Language Arts* 79 (4): 312–22.

Anderson, C. 2000. *How's It Going?: A Practical Guide to Conferring With Student Writers.* Portsmouth, NH: Heinemann.

Aud, S., W. Hussar, F. Johnson, G. Kena, E. Roth, E. Manning, X. Wang, and J. Zhang. 2012. *The Condition of Education 2012* (NCES 2012-045). Washington, D.C.: U.S. Department of Education, National Center for Education Statistics. Retrieved February 7, 2013. http://nces.ed.gov/programs/coe/pdf/coe_tsp.pdf and http://nces.ed.gov/programs/coe/indicator_ell.asp.

August, D., and T. Shanahan. 2006. *Developing Literacy in Second-Language Learners: Report of the National Literacy Panel on Language-Minority Children and Youth.* Mahwah, NJ: Lawrence Erlbaum Associates.

Barnes, D. 1992. *From Communication to Curriculum.* Second ed. Portsmouth, NH: Heinemann.

Bomer, R. 1995. *Time for Meaning.* Portsmouth, NH: Heinemann.

Bomer, R. 2007. "When writing leads: An activity-theoretic account of the literate activity of first graders stronger at writing than reading." In *56th Yearbook of the National Reading Conference,* eds. D. Wells Rowe, T. R. Jimenez, D. L. Compton, D. K. Dickinson, K. You, K. M. Leander, and J. Risko, 151–63. Oak Creek, WI: National Reading Conference.

Bomer, R. 2011. *Building Adolescent Literacy in Today's English Classroom.* Portsmouth, NH: Heinemann.

Bomer, R., and K. Bomer. 2001. *For a Better World: Reading and Writing for Social Action.* Portsmouth, NH: Heinemann.

Buly, M. R. 2010. *English Language Learners in Literacy Workshops.* Urbana, IL: National Council of Teachers of English.

Calkins, L. 1994. *The Art of Teaching Writing.* Portsmouth, NH: Heinemann.

Cambourne, B. 1995. "Toward an Educationally Relevant Theory of Literacy Learning: Twenty Years of Inquiry." *The Reading Teacher* 49 (3): 182–90.

Carey, S. 2007. *Working with English Language Learners: Answers to Teachers' Top Ten Questions.* Second ed. Portsmouth, NH: Heinemann.

Celic, C. M. 2009. *English Language Learners Day by Day K–6.* Portsmouth, NH: Heinemann.

Chomsky, C. 1971. "Write First, Read Later." *Journal of Early Childhood Literacy* 47 (6): 296–99.

Christensen, L. 2001. "Where I'm From: Inviting Student's Lives Into the Classroom." In *Rethinking Our Classrooms: Teaching for Equity and Social Justice.* Vol. 2. Milwaukee, WI: Rethinking Schools.

Cummins, J. 1996. *Negotiating Identities: Education for Empowerment in a Diverse Society.* Los Angeles, CA: California Association of Bilingual Education.

Delpit, L. 1988. "The Silenced Dialogue: Power and Pedagogy in Educating Other People's Children." *Harvard Education Review* 58 (3): 280–98.

Dragan, P. B. 2005. *A How-To Guide for Teaching English Language Learners.* Portsmouth, NH: Heinemann.

Edelsky, C., K. Smith, and C. Faltis. 2008. *Side-by-Side Learning: Exemplary Literacy Practices for English Learners and English Speakers in the Mainstream Classroom.* New York, NY: Scholastic.

Elbow, P. 2004. "Write First: Putting Writing Before Reading Is an Effective Approach to Teaching and Learning." *Educational Leadership* 62 (2): 8–14.

Espinosa, L. M. 2008. "Challenging Common Myths about Young English Language Learners. New York: Foundation for Child Development." Retrieved May 10, 2012. http://fcd-us.org/resources/challenging-common-myths-about-young-english-language-learners.

Flint, A. S., and T. T. Laman. 2012. "Where Poems Hide: Finding Reflective, Critical Spaces Inside Writing Workshop." *Theory into Practice* 51 (1): 12–19.

Foster, M. 2002. "Using Call and Response to Facilitate Language Master and Literacy Acquisition Among African American Students." Washington, D.C.: Center for Applied Linguistics. Retrieved October 1, 2012. www.cal.org/resources/digest/0204foster.html.

Freeman, D. E., and Y. S. Freeman. 2001. *Between Worlds: Access to Second Language Acquisition* Second ed. Portsmouth, NH: Heinemann.

Freeman, Y. S., and D. E. Freeman. 2006. *Teaching Reading and Writing in Spanish and English in Bilingual and Dual Language Classrooms.* Portsmouth, NH: Heinemann.

Freire, P. 2000. *Pedagogy of the Oppressed*, 30th Anniversary Edition. New York: Continuum.

Fu, D. 2009. *Writing Between Languages: How English Language Learners Make the Transition to Fluency.* Portsmouth, NH: Heinemann.

Gibbons, P. 2002. *Scaffolding Language / Scaffolding Learning: Teaching Second Language Learners in the Mainstream Classroom.* Portsmouth, NH: Heinemann.

Goldenberg, C. 2008. "Teaching English Language Learners: What the Research Does—and Does Not—Say." *American Educator* Summer 8–44.

Gonzalez, N., L. C. Moll, and C. Amanti. 2005. *Funds of Knowledge: Theorizing Practices in Households and Classrooms.* New York: Lawrence Erlbaum Associates.

Graves, D. 1983. *Writing: Teachers and Children at Work.* Portsmouth, NH: Heinemann.

Gregory, E., S. Long, and D. Volk. 2004. *Many Pathways to Literacy: Young Children's Learning with Siblings, Grandparents, Peers, and Communities.* New York: Routledge.

Gutiérrez, K., and M. F. Orellana. 2006. "The 'Problem' of English Learners: Constructing Genres of Difference." *Research in the Teaching of English* 40 (4): 502–08.

Heard, G. 1999. *Awakening the Heart: Exploring Poetry in Elementary and Middle School.* Portsmouth, NH: Heinemann.

Houk, F. A. 2005. *Supporting English Language Learners: A Guide for Teachers and Administrators.* Portsmouth, NH: Heinemann.

Hudelson, S. 1984. "Kan yu ret an rayt en Ingles: Children Become Literate in English as a Second Language." *TESOL Quarterly* 18 (2): 221–238.

Johnston, P. 2004. *Choice Words: How Our Language Affects Children's Learning.* Portland, ME: Stenhouse.

Johnston, P. H. 2012. *Opening Minds: Using Language to Change Lives.* Portland, ME: Stenhouse.

Krashen, S. 1982. *Principles and Practices in Second Language Acquisition.* New York: Pergamon Press.

Laman, T. T. 2004. "It's Not Like We're Just Playing: It's About Learning Stuff": A Critical Ethnography of Children's Social Practices During Literacy Learning. Bloomington, IN: Unpublished doctoral dissertation, Indiana University.

Laman, T. T. 2011. "The Functions of Talk in a Fourth-Grade Writing Workshop: Insights into Understanding." *Journal of Research in Childhood Education* 25(2): 133–44.

Laman, T. T., and K. Van Sluys. 2008. "Being and Becoming: Multilingual Writers' Practices." *Language Arts* 85(4): 265–74.

Larson, J. 1999. "Analyzing Participation Frameworks in Kindergarten Writing Activity: The Role of the Overhearer in Learning to Write." *Written Communication* 16(2): 225–57.

Lewison, M., C. Leland, and J. C. Harste. 2008. *Creating Critical Classrooms: K–8 Reading and Writing with an Edge.* New York: Lawrence Erlbaum Associates.

López-Robertson, J., S. Long, and K. Turner-Nash. 2010. "'Day of small beginnings': First Steps in Constructing Counter-Narratives of Young Children and their Families." *Language Arts* 88(2): 93–103.

Lyon, G. E. 1999. *Where I'm From: Where Poems Come From.* Spring, TX: Absey and Company.

Nieto, S. 2010. *Language, Culture, and Teaching: Critcal Perspectives,* Second ed. New York: Routledge.

Orellana, M. F., and K. Gutiérrez. 2006. "What's the problem? Constructing Different Genres for the Study of English Learners." *Research in the Teaching of English* 41(1): 118–23.

Orellana, M. F. and J. Reynolds. 2008. "Cultural Modeling: Leveraging Bilingual Skills for School Paraphrasing Tasks." *Reading Research Quarterly* 43 (1): 48–65.

Orozco, C. S., M. M. Suárez-Orozco, and I. Todorova. 2008. *Learning a New Land.* Cambridge, MA: Belknap Press of Harvard University Press.

Ray, K. W. 1999. *Wondrous Words: Writers and Writing in the Elementary Classroom.* Urbana, IL: National Council of Teachers of English.

———. 2001. *The Writing Workshop: Working Through the Hard Parts (And They're All Hard Parts).* Urbana, IL: National Council of Teachers of English.

Ray, K. W. and L. Cleaveland. 2004. *About the Authors: Writing Workshop with Our Youngest Writers.* Portsmouth, NH: Heinemann.

Reyes, M. D. ed. 2011. *Words Were All We Had: Becoming Biliterate Against the Odds.* New York: Teachers College Press.

Robertson, J. L., S. Long, and K. Turner-Nash. 2010. "First Steps in Constructing Counter Narratives of Young Children and their Families." *Language Arts* 88(2): 93–104.

Rueda, R., D. August, and C. Goldenberg. 2006. "The Sociocultural Context in which Children Acquire Literacy." In *Developing Literacy in Second-Language Learners: Report of the National Literacy Panel on Language-Minority Children and Youth,* eds. D. August and T. Shanahan. Mahwah, NJ: Lawrence Erlbaum Associates.

Salomone, R. C. 2010. *True American: Language, Identity, and the Education of Immigrant Children.* Cambridge, MA: Harvard University Press.

Samway, K. 2006. *When English Language Learners Write.* Portsmouth, NH: Heinemann.

Samway, K., and D. McKeon. 1999. *Myths and Realities: Best Practices for Language Minority Students.* Portsmouth, NH: Heinemann.

Schatz, M., and L. C. Wilkinson. 2012. *Understanding Language in Diverse Classrooms: A Primer for All Teachers.* New York: Routledge.

Short, K., J. C. Harste, and C. Burke. 1996. *Creating Classrooms for Authors and Inquirers,* Second ed. Portsmouth, NH: Heinemann.

Smitherman, G. 1985. *Talkin and Testifyin: The Language of Black America.* Detroit, IL: Wayne State University Press.

Soltero, S. W. 2011. *Schoolwide Approaches to Educating English Language Learners.* Portsmouth, NH: Heinemann.

Street, B. 1995. *Social Literacies: Critical Approaches to Literacy in Development, Ethnography, and Education.* New York: Longman.

Suárez-Orozco, C., M. M. Suárez-Orozco, and I. Todorova. 2008. *Learning a New Land: Immigrant Students in American Society.* Cambridge, MA: Harvard University Press.

Tucker, G. R. 2009. "A Global Perspective on Bilingualism and Bilingual Education." Retrieved November 12, 2011. www.cal.org/resources/Digest/digestglobal.html.

Van Sluys, K. 2003. Writing and Identity Construction: A Young Author's Life in Transition. *Language Arts* 80 (3): 176–84.

Vasquez, V. 2004. *Negotiating Critical Literacies with Young Children.* New York: Routledge.

Wenger, E. 1998. *Communities of Practice: Learning, Meaning, and Identity.* New York: Cambridge University Press.

Index

Houk, F. A., 16
Hudelson, S., 5
Hughes, Langston, 123

Ideas, demonstrate, 47
Identity
    awareness of multilingual, 143
    building an, 65
    engagement and, 64–65
    as learning vehicle, 11
    recognizing, 98–100
    as writer, 98
    writing conference and, 94–95
Illustrations
    reinforce new language with, 47
    scaffold communication with, 89–92
    See also Drawing; Picture
Immersion, as engagement, 64
Independent writing time
    build skills during, 73–76
    immersion and, 64
    need for, 66–67
    writing conference during, 83–84
    writing in multiple languages during,
        70–72
    in writing workshop, 7
Indiana Partnership for Young Writers, 126
In My Family / En mi familia (Garza), 47, 48
Inquiry, during minilesson, 52
Inspiration, writing conference and, 97
Interest inventory, 27, 157–158
Isoke, N., 83

Jackson, Kyleen, 27, 96, 119, 123
Javier (fourth grader), 61, 106, 132, 146–151
Johnston, P., 15, 64–65, 70, 94

Kelly, Theresa, 47, 99–100, 118, 119
Kingsolver, Barbara, 9
Krashen, S., 16

Labels
    integrate first languages using, 21–23
    listening for content, not correction, to
        teach, 92–94
    multilingual, 21
    in multiple languages, for drawings, 72
Laman, T. T., 5, 22, 70, 120, 127
Language lessons
    as minilesson category, 58
    possible, 61–62
Languages
    writing in multiple, as asset, 119
    See also First language; Primary language
Languages in classrooms
    build library, 25–26
    integrate first languages using labels, 21–23
    share families' first-language experiences,
        23–24
Large-scale projects, 129
Larson, J., 86
Learning
    conditions of, 50
    immersion as "essential condition" of, 64
LEP. *See* Limited English Proficient
Library, multilingual, multicultural, 25–26
Limited English Proficient (LEP), 2
Lisa (kindergartener), 92–94
Listening during writing conference, 85–94
    for content, not correction, 85–86, 92–94
    facilitate communication, 86–89
    go to the children, 86–87
    observe before speaking, 86